SPOUT SPRING
A Black Community

By

PETER KUNKEL AND SARA SUE KENNARD

St. Ambrose College

HOLT, RINEHART AND WINSTON, INC.

NEW YORK   CHICAGO   SAN FRANCISCO   ATLANTA   DALLAS

MONTREAL   TORONTO   LONDON   SYDNEY

Cover: *A street in Spout Spring.*
Boy walking from school
to his grandparents' house.
Photograph by Roy Brophy.

Foreword

About the Book

Spout Spring is a case study of a kind of Black community in the United States about which relatively little has been written. It is in many ways the antithesis of the inner-city Black ghetto. It is a stable community and its people are relatively secure economically. This is not to say that the income level is high or that life in Spout Spring is without vexation. Many of the problems that plague and obstruct Blacks elsewhere as they strive to improve their situation are present in some form in Spout Spring.

This case study is an ethnography. Descriptive and low key, it is neither interpretive nor strongly theoretical in orientation. The people and their situation come on in a direct personal way. The significance of this ethnography is that the community described is an important variation in the relationship of Blacks to White-dominated society. In the face of dramatic confrontations elsewhere, a community like Spout Spring, and the life it represents, is easily overlooked.

One theme of this case study is integration vs. separatism. Some young Blacks in Spout Spring are attracted to the idea of separate Black institutions. In sharp contrast, most older people are still cautiously committed to the idea that true integration will sooner or later prove possible. A few older leaders, however, are ambivalent about integration as an alternative to an accommodationist type of separatism; they realize that consolidation of their organizations with White organizations may result in elimination of their own leadership roles. As the authors point out, the older institutions of Spout Spring are on the whole accommodationist, not reformative, and certainly not revolutionary in their orientation. Newer institutions are cautiously but persistently assimilationist.

Sequoyah, the larger community of which Spout Spring is a part, is changing. Some of the barriers between Blacks and Whites are breaking down. The university community in particular has worked to open significant doors to integration. These developments are accompanied by educational integration and some improvement in employment opportunities for Blacks. The Sequoyah–Spout Spring environment will be different in the future than it has been in the past and, from the point of view of those interested in integration and civil rights, it will be better. It will probably not change enough to satisfy the aspiration of all members of the Black community. Nevertheless, the differences between present conditions (1965–1970) and those that characterized the period before World War II are at least mildly encouraging.

GEORGE AND LOUISE SPINDLER
General Editors

Phlox, Wisconsin

About the Authors

Peter Kunkel was born in Davenport, Iowa. Except for three years in Chicago during his junior high school years, he grew up and was educated in Davenport. He joined the United States Navy in 1936, served three enlistments, and received his final discharge in 1947. Naval service included a tour of duty with the old Asiatic Fleet (1936–1938), wartime assignments with naval armed guard units on merchant ships (1942-1945), and participation in the Bikini atom bomb tests of 1946. At the conclusion of his naval service, Kunkel held the petty officer rating of Boatswain's Mate, First Class.

After leaving the Navy, Kunkel enrolled at the University of New Mexico. There he discovered anthropology. As an anthropology major he took the following degrees: BA at the University of New Mexico (1951), MA (1954) and PhD (1962) at the University of California at Los Angeles. He has taught at the University of Richmond, Virginia, Los Angeles State College, Humboldt State College, the University of Arkansas, the University of Tulsa, and East Carolina University. He is currently Associate Professor and Chairman of the Sociology Department at Saint Ambrose College in Davenport, Iowa.

Dr. Kunkel has tended to generalize as an anthropologist, both in teaching and in research. His research interests have included California Indian ecology and political systems, archaeological field work in New Mexico, Iowa, California, Mexico, eastern Tennessee, and eastern North Carolina and ethnological surveys in Mexico. Most of these activities were carried out in the interests of research programs of other anthropologists. After a period of residence and research in "western Ozarka," Kunkel now seeks to specialize in the study of modern ethnic and regional subcultures in the United States, with emphasis on Black and Ozark subcultures.

Sara Sue Kennard (Mrs. Kunkel) is a "natural ethnographer" in the tradition of Matilda Coxe Stevenson, Curt Nimuendaju, Robert Weitlaner, and Robert Spott. She was born in Beggs, Oklahoma, grew up in Oklahoma City and was educated in the schools of that city. During World War II she served in the Women's Army Corps and was stationed in Hawaii. Since the war she has lived and worked in various parts of the United States. More than ten years of that time have been spent in Ozarka and nearby states. Her experience, in work and business, have given her opportunities to be a participant observer of Ozark and near-Ozark life in a wide variety of roles. She brought insights from her background in the region to this book, providing much needed critical perspective.

Preface

The Spout Spring neighborhood is a real community; only its name is fictitious. Each individual discussed in this book represents a composite of actual characteristics and life circumstances, though real names have not been used and some particulars have been altered to protect identities. The name of the state (Ozarka) is, of course, fictitious, as are the names of the county (Lincoln) and the city (Sequoyah).

Our opportunity to know the people of Spout Spring, the Black community of Sequoyah, came during a five-year period of intermittent residence in the city and county. It began in 1964, when I came to teach at Ozarka University. I began to meet Black people through volunteer work for two social-action organizations: first, the Sequoyah Good Neighbor Council (SGNC) and, later, the Lincoln County Community Outreach Agency (COA). The SGNC is a moderate, biracial, civil rights organization; the COA is the local, federally funded, anti-poverty agency.

Sara Sue Kennard has had considerable contacts with Ozark people, Black and White, in Ozarka and in other states. She has contributed to this book on many levels. Initially she was an "informant" on aspects of White regional subculture. Later she did research on historical background and critically read early drafts of the book. Finally, she wrote or rewrote certain chapters or parts of chapters. For instance she was especially involved in writing Chapter 3 (*The Knight Family*), the section of Chapter 8 entitled *Music and Dance*, and various parts of the earlier chapters (to Chapter 5).

We wish to acknowledge Mr. Albert Niblack's contribution to the initial planning of this book. Mr. Niblack is a long-time resident of west Ozarka. He collaborated with me on several of the original projects undertaken for the SGNC and COA. We regret that other interests claimed his attention, preventing him from participating as co-author in the writing of this book.

The Black people of Sequoyah have also contributed to this book in a very creative way. Of course, many individuals supplied data in interviews but, beyond that, a number of the Sequoyah people were asked to read or listen to early drafts of the book. Their comments and suggestions are reflected in the final writing.

Thus, we are speaking *for* the Black community of Sequoyah—not just about it. We collaborated closely with many of its members in community projects. Much of our personal lives, and a great deal of time, were tied up with these projects and with the people involved in them. Our associates have been kind and friendly to us.

It is a paradox of ethnography that the frank expression of interest in *writing* about a community can result in the creation of barriers to free communication. Where relationships are completely personal, without concern for writing or reporting, communication is less inhibited. This problem was evident in the Spout Spring neighborhood when we announced to our friends that we were going to write a book about them. Here, however, our social-action work, for which we had written reports about the community, stood us in good stead. Our friendships continued and our friends were willing to help us understand themselves and their community, but our authors' role probably inhibited many other people who did not know us so well. Because of a natural desire to have the book show the community in a favorable light, they doubtless censored some information and value judgments. But more often, however, the people of Spout Spring displayed a strong desire that a true and total picture of the community be presented.

Thus, in the long run, there came to be a feeling among Spout Spring people that this book was *their* book, *their* statement to the world about themselves. There is the obvious danger that the ethnographer's close relationship and identification with the people he writes about may compromise his objectivity. We feel that the insights outweigh the risk.

There are holes in our data. We simply do not have enough information about some areas of Spout Spring life. Our knowledge of the religious side of life is superficial, and we do not know enough about what social psychologists call "deviant behavior." There are doubtless other gaps, gaps of which we are not even aware. We acknowledge these lacunae as matters of fact, not as an apology. The circumstances under which we worked forced us to make hard choices on how to make use of limited resources of time and money. Throughout the period of research and writing it was necessary to be concerned with making a living.

The Executive Director, Board of Directors, and staff members of the "Lincoln County Community Outreach Agency" have been most generous in letting us use facilities and records of the agency for research purposes. This, at a time when the agency was very controversial and hence vulnerable to criticism from conflicting interest groups in Lincoln County.

Dr. Barry Kinsey, Chairman of the Department of Sociology and Anthropology, University of Tulsa, was most considerate in arranging my teaching schedule during the fall semester of 1968–1969 to allow a maximum amount of time for field work in Sequoyah.

President Leo Jenkins of East Carolina University and Dr. Melvin Williams of that university's Department of Sociology and Anthropology showed great patience and generosity in giving me leave of absence for two academic quarters in 1968 and 1969.

Colleagues at the University of Arkansas contributed in many ways to our understanding of research problems in Sequoyah and its Black community.

The photographs were taken by Sara Sue Kennard; Roy Brophy, anthropology major at East Carolina University; and Ray Medlock, graduate anthropology major at the University of Arkansas.

Ruth Chapman, Editor at Holt, Rinehart and Winston, contributed numerous suggestions which have improved the style and flow of our narrative.

To all of these persons and institutions we express our deep gratitude. We reserve for ourselves, alone, responsibility for inadequacies or errors in data or interpretation.

PETER KUNKEL
SARA SUE KENNARD

Contents

1

Sequoyah and Its Black Community

S EQUOYAH IS A CITY in the western part of the state of Ozarka. Its population, of about 25,000 includes slightly more than six hundred Black people. Some of these are students at Ozarka State University. The rest, the permanent Black residents, constitute what we will call the Sequoyah Black community.

In using the term "Black" in the preceding paragraph, we follow current nationwide preference. However, Black people in Sequoyah still seem to find "Negro" at least equally acceptable. Perhaps this is a case of "cultural lag." Be that as it may, the Black people of Sequoyah know who they are and how they came to be where they are. So do the Whites with whom and for whom they work. But both Blacks and Whites in this area tend to concern themselves with people as individuals rather than categories, at least when they are dealing with them personally. In this book we will have to make fairly frequent reference to racial categories. In doing so, we will follow local usage in the Black community—using Negro and Black interchangeably. For the principal contrasting racial entity we will use White.

At present* the Sequoyah Black community consists of about 460 permanent residents, most of whom live within a twelve-block area on the east side of the city. This area is locally known as the Spout Spring neighborhood.

Despite the residential concentration of Sequoyah Negroes, their daily activities take most of them to all parts of the city. Like all other residents of Sequoyah, they are subject to municipal ordinances, pay city taxes, vote in city elections, and send their children to city schools, which are now completely desegregated in a formal sense, though by no means in a social sense. In short, the Black population of Sequoyah is very much involved in the total community. Their past is part of the history of Sequoyah and of Lincoln County. Therefore,

---

* When we speak of the present, we refer to September, 1968, when this study was completed. All figures refer to this date unless otherwise specified.

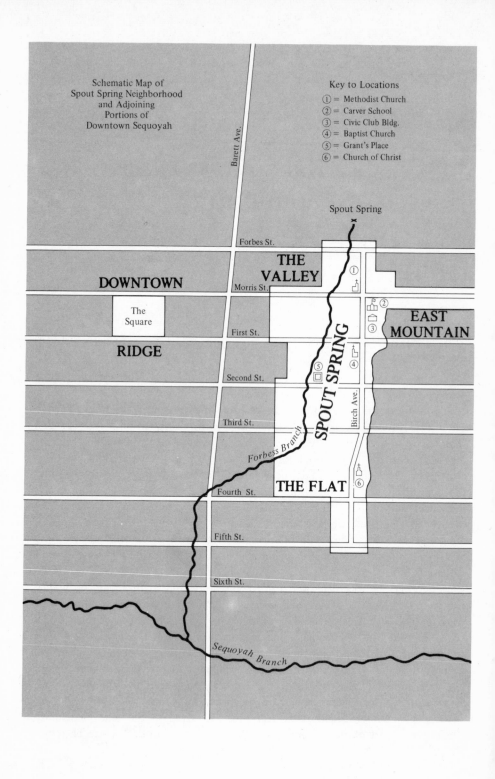

Schematic Map of
Spout Spring Neighborhood
and Adjoining
Portions of
Downtown Sequoyah

Key to Locations
① = Methodist Church
② = Carver School
③ = Civic Club Bldg.
④ = Baptist Church
⑤ = Grant's Place
⑥ = Church of Christ

Barett Ave.

Spout Spring

Forbes St.

DOWNTOWN

THE
VALLEY

Morris St.

①

The
Square

First St.

②
③

EAST
MOUNTAIN

RIDGE

④

Second St.

⑤

Third St.

SPOUT SPRING

Birch Ave.

Forbess Branch

THE FLAT

⑥

Fourth St.

Fifth St.

Sixth St.

Sequoyah Branch

some knowledge of Sequoyah and of Lincoln County is necessary to an understanding of this Black community.

The View from East Mountain

The city of Sequoyah is built on a series of ridges. The highest of these is East Mountain, which lies on the east side of the city. On top of East Mountain is an oval, relatively level plateau, from which there is a dramatic view westward across town. From this vantage point one sees a sequence of three other ridges, one behind the other. All three trend in a north-south direction and are connected by lower, east-west trending ridges. These ridges, and East Mountain, are all remnants of an old plateau, now much worn down by its stream drainages.

Between the southern flank of East Mountain and the first lateral ridge to the west lies one of the smaller valleys produced by the plateau's erosion. The principal erosional agent, here, has been a small stream, Forbes Branch, which carries water from several springs on the side of East Mountain. The most important of these is Spout Spring, near the junction of Forbes Street and Birch Avenue. The little valley is about a half-mile in length, starting high and narrow at its northern end, above Spout Spring, and sloping sharply down to an alluvial fan spilling out onto a broad plain at its southern end. For most of its length, the valley is narrow and steeply sloped on both sides, though it widens a bit toward its mouth. Packed snugly into the southern portion of this valley, from Spout Spring south, are the houses of the Sequoyah Black community.

The ridge west of the Forbes Branch valley is much lower than East Mountain but is also capped by a level plateau. On this plateau lies the Square and the old "Downtown" of Sequoyah. In a second valley, west of the Downtown ridge, are the tracks of the St. Louis and San Francisco Railroad (the "Frisco Line") passing through the heart of the city. Beyond this valley is another ridge, the University ridge. Here lies the main campus of Ozarka State University and residential areas peripheral to it.

Beyond the University ridge is a third, broader valley, which is occupied by the university's football stadium, athletic practice fields, and university-owned housing units. West of this valley, the third ridge is an area of scattered suburban residences with intervening woods.

Across the south side of the city, there is a wide, flat valley, which is broken by some minor elevations. This valley runs from east to west. Into it slope the southern flanks of East Mountain and the two other ridges just described. A similar broad valley runs from east to west across the north end of Sequoyah. The southern transverse valley carries streams that flow south and east toward the Elk River. The northern transverse valley carries streams that flow north and west toward the Osage River. Hills at the west end of the southern valley and at the east end of the northern valley join with the complex high ground of Sequoyah to form the watershed between the two rivers' drainages. The rivers have long ago scoured deeply into the old plateau, and their tributary streams have transformed the remaining portions into the complex of hills, ridges, and valleys that can be seen from East Mountain. It is this process that has created the distinctive landscape of western Ozarka. The result is a region of impressive beauty but relatively poor fertility, except for valley bottom lands, where soils eroded off the higher ground have been deposited. Although the trend of the Elk-Osage watershed is east-west in the Sequoyah locality, the general trend is south-north, following the general trend of the courses of the two rivers.

The Growth Pattern of Sequoyah

The city of Sequoyah began with the construction of two log houses near Spout Spring. Pioneer John Forbes built the two houses 140 years ago. As the community grew, the center of growth shifted to the Downtown ridge, where the Square developed.

Early growth of the city was slow and mainly toward the north. With the founding of the university in 1880, expansion toward the west began. Soon afterward the railroad came through, and then a lumber boom stimulated the development of lumber mills and yards in the valley south of town, with housing for mill employees in that area. Ever since, the southern end of Sequoyah has been predominantly an area of working-class residences, interspersed with industry and business.

Early twentieth-century growth of the city saw expansion in all directions; but since World War II there has been especially rapid growth to the north, northeast, and northwest. In general, middle- and upper-class families have clustered in neighborhoods on higher ground and toward the northern, eastern, and western edges of town. The best neighborhoods today are on East Mountain and on associated highland formations.

Although poor neighborhoods tend to be toward the south and on low ground, they are not exclusively located there. Moreover, there are no neighborhoods that are completely "poor"; that is, lower-middle- and upper-lower-class families are usually found intermixed with poorer families in such neighborhoods.

The economically heterogeneous character of certain "poverty neighborhoods" in Sequoyah was demonstrated in 1967 by a community self-survey sponsored by the local anti-poverty agency, the Lincoln County Community Outreach Agency (COA). The self-survey group selected certain blocks scattered throughout the city as likely "poverty concentrations." Their selections were based on housing conditions in the blocks, as classified by the city's planning consultant and his staff. Results of the COA survey indicated that (a) 39.2 percent of the households had annual incomes below national Office of Economic Opportunity (OEO) poverty-defining guidelines, (b) 29.5 percent of the households were borderline cases of "fringe poverty" (that is, had annual incomes within $1000 more than the OEO guidelines), and (c) 31.3 percent of the households were definitely above the poverty level.

The Spout Spring neighborhood was not one of those covered by the 1967 self-survey. However, we have since determined that poverty runs about 5 percent higher there. That is, 44 percent of the Black households are in the poverty category, as compared to 39.2 percent of the households in the self-survey blocks.

The Spout Spring Neighborhood

There is a tradition that Negroes once lived around the Square and also along Barrett Avenue, the principal north-south street of Sequoyah. Their concentration into the valley of Forbes Branch seems to be relatively recent. However, some Negroes apparently began to settle in that area during the latter half of the nineteenth century. The earlier pattern of widespread residence occurred because certain Negro families lived close by the homes of well-to-do White families for whom they worked as servants. The lifelong family servant is no longer an important phenomenon, and the change in settlement pattern is related to this fact. However, the growth of the present Black neighborhood represents an in-gathering of former rural Negro families more that it does a shift in residence pattern on the part of older urban Negro families. Most of today's Black families can be traced to rural areas of Lincoln County several generations back. There are a few families whose Sequoyah residence clearly goes back to the nineteenth century, but most "old Negro families" have apparently died out or moved away.

Negro settlement in the Forbes Branch valley originally clustered near Spout Spring, which was the source of water for the houses in the settlement. Spring water was carried in buckets for most household uses. And there was always a tin cup hanging from a branch by the stream for anyone who wished to take a drink of the cool water. Thus the unity of the little settlement was based on the water source, and its name came to identify the community as it grew.

The Negroes of Lincoln County

Today there are few Negroes in Lincoln County outside of the city of Sequoyah. Moreover, the Sequoyah Black community is the only substantial cluster of Negroes in western Ozarka. During the present century many towns in this region have discouraged Negroes from settling. In many smaller western Ozarka towns, it was not uncommon, even as late as the 1950s, to see signs warning Negroes not to stay in town past sundown. This contrasts with the situation during the late nineteenth century, when rural portions of Lincoln County did have a considerable Black component, although always as a minority of the total population. To a lesser extent, neighboring counties also had Negroes living in the countryside or in small towns.

Blacks were first brought into Lincoln County to work as field hands on farms. Before the Civil War they were concentrated in the western part of the county, in the Osage River drainage, which drew a majority of the settlers in early days. These settlers were mostly Cumberland Presbyterians from Tennessee, who introduced the typical Southern plantation concept, based on large land holdings worked by gangs of slaves. The Osage drainage seems to have been one of the few places in western Ozarka where this economic pattern was feasible. In 1850 there were 279 slaves in Rush Hill Township (twenty miles from Sequoyah); adjacent Morris Township had 325. These two townships alone accounted for nearly half of the Black population of the county, which then totaled 1213. However, the White population exceeded the Black population in both these townships.

Many Black families of Sequoyah trace their origins back to Rush Hill. Negroes who worked as slaves on plantations of the Rush Hill area in pre-Civil War days later acquired lands of their own (in some cases bequeathed to them in the wills of former masters) or became sharecroppers. The last families to leave Rush Hill to move into Sequoyah did so in the years right after World War II. Today only one elderly Negro couple remains in Rush Hill, while one elderly Negro man lives in the nearby town of Morris.

Population

The first census of Lincoln County was taken in 1830. It listed 233 "heads of families," which suggests a total population of perhaps a thousand. Of these, more than one hundred were Negro slaves. The 1840 Census enumerated 6246 Whites and 625 Negroes in the county, of which 292 Whites and 123 Blacks lived in Sequoyah. Three of these Blacks were listed as freemen; 120 were slaves.

The Negro population of Lincoln County reached its peak in 1860, when the census records 1538 "colored persons." The total county population at this time was about 15,000. The population of Sequoyah, then, was around 3000, of whom 294 were Negro slaves employed as house servants, artisans, or laborers. After the Civil War the Negro population of Sequoyah increased, reaching 330 by the year 1870, although the total Negro population of the county dropped to 674. This marked the beginning of a steady migration of Black people from rural areas of the county into Sequoyah. This migration did not really stop in Sequoyah. While rural Negroes have been gradually moving into Sequoyah, the Negroes of Sequoyah have, in turn, been moving to northern and western cities of larger size.

Since 1870 the Black population of Sequoyah has tended to fluctuate both seasonally and over a period of years. In the pattern of long-term fluctuation, it reached its low point in the 1920s, when about 200 Black residents are recorded. By way of contrast, Black leaders report a high point of over 1000 at some unspecified earlier period. We are inclined to view this figure as somewhat exaggerated but feel that it may reflect a pre-World War I population peak of between 500 and 1000. Within the past decade estimates or census counts have run from 400 to 600.

We worked up our own estimate of the permanent Black population of Sequoyah in September, 1968. The total figure derived was 460. Of these, 445 lived in the Spout Spring neighborhood, while 15 lived elsewhere in the city. We also estimated the number of temporary Black residents of Sequoyah to be about 150. Most of these, perhaps all, were students living in university housing. Within the Spout Spring neighborhood we identified 117 households occupying 110 houses. These households included 120 adult males and 130 adult females. We have only partial data on children, but we estimate that there were about 195. If anything, our estimate errs on the conservative side, because it refers to the month of September. We believe that the midsummer population tends to be larger than that during other seasons. At that time many families have out-of-town kinfolks staying with them. These are usually former residents who have come back "home" for vacation visits.

Long-term population fluctuation is much influenced by the fact that individuals who move away often come back years later and re-establish residence. Some people also commute between a Spout Spring home base and job opportunities elsewhere. Boys leave to join the armed services. Some of them come back after serving their enlistments; others find jobs elsewhere and are lost to the local population, at least for a while. It is noteworthy that most Black men have served in the armed services at some time or other. At least ten young men were on active duty in the fall of 1968. In addition, there are two Army career men: one, a sergeant, maintains a home in Sequoyah, where his wife and children live; the other, a lieutenant-colonel, probably does not now consider Sequoyah to be his home although his father and mother still live there.

Black-White Relations

The population of Sequoyah has doubled and redoubled in the last thirty years. In 1940 it was still just a college town, with fewer than 10,000 people. Today it is a rapidly growing city of above 25,000. This fourfold expansion included many families from other parts of the United States—from the East, West, and North, as well as from other parts of the South. Most of these have been middle-class families, drawn to the university, to managerial or professional opportunities in business or industry, or to retirement in an attractive four-seasons environment.

Expanded industry has also drawn poor White people from the nearby hinterlands. Most of them come from rural Lincoln County or from adjacent counties, but some come from nearby states, attracted to unskilled or semiskilled wage-work in food-processing plants or other industry in Sequoyah. When these Whites first come to the city, they are inclined to be vaguely anti-Negro, but when they actually come into contact with Blacks in work situations, many of them get along pretty well with them. Their initial attitudes contrast considerably with those of most middle-class newcomers, who tend to have sympathetic predispositions toward the Black population.

Culturally the Sequoyah Negroes are more like the transplanted rural and small-town working-class Whites than like the middle-class newcomers. They share many traits, attitudes, and beliefs with the other natives of the region as well as with the inmigrating rural people. We will discuss aspects of the shared regional western Ozarka subculture in Chapter 8.

Sequoyah Blacks share another subculture with their poor White neighbors and co-workers, namely, that of poverty.

Poverty: Black and White

The Spout Spring neighborhood lies within a larger area of lower-class housing, which the Housing Authority has designated the Birch Avenue district. This is one of the two areas of Sequoyah that are locally regarded as the poorest sections of town. The other reputed intensive-poverty area is the West End district, a smaller, exclusively White neighborhood in the southwest part of Sequoyah. The West End district has been designated a target area of poverty by the County COA. So has the Birch Avenue District. Recent social surveys in these two target areas indicate that they are economically more heterogeneous than had been supposed. Nevertheless, these surveys do indicate that a majority of families in both areas have incomes below $5000 a year.

The seventy-five houses in the West End district were surveyed in 1966 by the city's Housing Authority. Results of this survey showed that 46.6 percent of the households in the district had annual incomes below $3000. The Housing Authority also surveyed 217 White and Black households along Birch Avenue and in blocks immediately east and west, within the Birch Avenue district. The results of this survey indicate that 47.9 percent of the households had annual incomes below $3000. Since the Housing Authority did not report its Birch Avenue results in terms of a breakdown between Black and White categories of households, we conducted another survey of income in the summer of 1968 for 84 Black households in the Birch Avenue district. Most or all of these households were probably among those previously surveyed by the Housing Authority. Our survey found that 44.0 percent of the households had annual incomes below $3000. The findings of the three surveys are summarized in the following table.

	Percentage of Income		
SURVEY	Below $3,000	$3,000–$5,000	Above $5,000
West End (1966)	46.6	37.3	16.1
Birch Ave. (1966)	47.9	31.8	20.3
Birch Ave. Blacks (1968)	44.0	28.6	27.4

This comparison suggests that the Black community has slightly less poverty than Whites in either the West End or the Birch Avenue districts. Moreover, the number of Black families with incomes above $5000 per year is significantly higher than for White families in the two districts. However, there may have been more income available in 1968 than in 1966; we have some reason to believe that Black incomes in Sequoyah may have increased selectively during the two-year period.

A similar picture is revealed by another comparison. This is made possible because some of the blocks in the Birch Avenue district that were not included in the Housing Authority survey of 1966 were included in the COA self-survey of 1967 (see p. 4). The COA survey covered a total of 73 households in this area, all of them White. The data on these 73 households were pulled out and analyzed separately by COA staff members in the summer of 1969 and can be compared to data on the 84 Black households surveyed by us in 1968. In both cases the data have been analyzed in terms of national OEO sliding-scale guidelines, which vary with the number of persons in a family. This yields different figures than the static Housing and Urban Development (HUD) guidelines used by the Housing Authority (and by us in the comparison summarized in the preceding table). The following table summarizes the results of our second analysis:

	Percentage Rate		
SURVEY	Poverty	Fringe Poverty	Above Poverty
Birch Ave. Whites (1967)	41.1	34.2	24.7
Birch Ave. Blacks (1968)	44.0	27.4	28.6

Although the differences are less marked in this comparison (which involves a time gap of only about one year), we note a higher percentage of Black families in *both* the Poverty and the Above-Poverty categories, with a higher percentage of White households in the Fringe-Poverty category.

The general conclusion one derives from analyzing the data from these surveys is that the Black residential area, like most old Sequoyah neighborhoods with predominantly "substandard" housing ratings, is an economically heterogeneous neighborhood. Despite this economic heterogeneity most of the Black people, like their White neighbors, are either poor or on the borderline of poverty. There is some reason to believe that Black people use their money more efficiently than Whites in the same general economic levels. For instance, according to the Housing Authority report of 1966, 45 percent of the families of the West End district owned their own homes. But according to our survey of the Spout Spring neighborhood, in 1968, 60 percent of the families own their own homes. Observations on maintenance and upkeep also lend support to this conclusion. We attribute this difference to the greater sophistication of these urban Black people, most of whom have lived much longer in Sequoyah than the average White family in the comparison groups.

Most poor Whites in Sequoyah are recently transplanted rural people. The semisubsistence country economy that once supported them in a frugal but self-respecting way of life has been gradually disappearing during the past thirty years. At one time Negroes also participated in the traditional rural economy, but their share in it broke down earlier; hence their moves to the city took place earlier. Moreover, when each family moved into Sequoyah, it found that there was a well-established economic role for Black people. In a sense, Blacks have held a near-monopoly on certain service occupations, and they have learned how to exploit this situation in a very sophisticated manner. This monopoly is now breaking down, but so is the job barrier that previously set limits on the kinds of work Blacks could do.

Spout Spring's Settlement Pattern

Despite cultural and economic similarities to many native Whites, the Black people of Sequoyah form a distinct community within the city. They are set apart by their color and by their residential situation, as well as by their greater adaptation to city life. The "colored district" is narrow, irregular in outline, and about a half-mile long—north to south. The southern portion is not completely segregated.

The Spout Spring neighborhood really consists of two somewhat distinct subneighborhoods. One is the Valley, in the little Forbes Branch drainage north of the old Morganton Road. The other part is the Flat, which lies south of the Morganton Road.

The Valley is a concentrated neighborhood, which grew up immediately south of Spout Spring. Most Sequoyah Black people live there, nearly 400 people in 90 houses. Households range in size from one to twelve members. The physical dimensions of the Valley can be stated as four blocks in a north-south direction by two blocks in an east-west direction. These are approximate figures; blocks are difficult to define clearly in the Valley. Moreover, the settlement pattern is not a neat rectangle. It bulges. Black residence extends farther on some streets than on others.

The Flat used to be called Newton's Flat, after a prominent Black family that once owned most of the land down there. But usage has shortened its name. The Flat refers only to the little alluvial fan deposited by Forbes Branch at the mouth of the Valley, not to the whole large plain lying on the south side of the city.

Mrs. Daphne Newton, a lifelong resident of the neighborhood, tells us that the Flat has always been a mixed residential area, desegregated, with both White and Black families in residence. Until about twenty years ago it was semirural, with widely dispersed residences. Intervening fields were devoted to truck gardening or to the pasturage of domestic animals. Today it is more compactly settled, and food production is less important, although several families still maintain gardens and at least one family still keeps livestock. The area of Black residence here is smaller and less densely settled than the Valley. There are twenty-one Black households in the Flat, ranging in size from one to six persons. Altogether, sixty-two persons are members of these households.

Most of the streets of Spout Spring are paved but lack curbs. All of them are flanked by open ditches and there are no sidewalks. Birch Avenue ties the neighborhood together. It runs from north to south with a gradually descending gradient along the side of the lower slope of East Mountain, then drops sharply to cross the Morganton Road, beyond which it continues, sloping very slightly, into the Flat.

In the Valley, Birch Avenue is intersected by four east-west streets: Morris, First, Second, and Third. Each is a very old Sequoyah street. West of the Valley, well-paved, curbed versions of these streets cross the Downtown ridge. Morris and First streets form the north and south sides of Sequoyah's Square. East of the ridge, Morris, First, and Second drop off into the Valley—where First ceases to be paved—then climb to dead ends part way up the side of East Mountain. Third Street drops off the Downtown ridge into the Flat and carries the Old Morganton Road out of town to the east. It is the southern boundary of the Valley.

South of the Valley, Birch Avenue continues for two more blocks, ending at its juncture with Fifth Street. The mixed residence pattern already mentioned is found along this stretch of Birch, as well as on Fourth and Fifth streets near their intersections with Birch. All three of these streets are paved; Fourth and Fifth have curbs. White housing is found continuously to the east and west of this little suburb of Spout Spring.

Despite the physically semidetatched location of the Flat, Spout Spring is one neighborhood, not two. Its people form one community in which almost everybody knows everybody. Most people are bound together in a network of kin ties traced equally on both male and female sides. Incest concepts prevent marriages within the range of first cousins, and there is a tendency to feel that marriages should not occur too frequently between people with the same two family names. Nevertheless, marriages take place more often within than without this local population of between 450 and 500. When people die, they are usually buried in the segregated Elms Cemetery, which is located about a half-mile southeast of the Black residential area. This little Negro cemetery is maintained, and apparently owned, by the Civic Club, an organization that seeks to represent the common interests of the Black people of Sequoyah.

The Valley is the real heart of the Spout Spring community. It has most of the Black population and most of the Black social institutions: the old Carver School, the Methodist Church, the Baptist Church, the Civic Club building—and the tavern known as Grant's Place.

2

The View from Grant's Place

THE ONLY BLACK-OWNED AND CONTROLLED BUSINESS enterprise in the Spout Spring neighborhood is a tavern, the Second Street Club. There is no sign to identify it as such, and it is generally known in the community and throughout Sequoyah by the given name of its proprietor as Grant's Place. This is how Grant's Place came to be.

Grant's Odyssey

In the spring of 1942, a young man named Grant Barbour left Spout Spring to join the Navy. In the Navy he was trained as a cook. But, later, while serving on an LST in the Pacific, he changed his rating from Ship's Cook to Ship-fitter. "That's not an easy thing to do in the Navy—to change your rating, if you're a petty officer. But I was such a bad cook they was willin' to do anythin' to get me out o' the galley. And I guess they figured I'd do better gettin' rid of the garbage than dishing it out. You know what a shipfitter's for, don't you? He keeps a ship's plumbing runnin' right."

After the war Grant Barbour returned to Sequoyah for about a year. During that year he took some vocational courses and held a few jobs, none of which paid as much as he'd been making in the Navy as a petty officer, second class. He wanted to get into plumbing work, then, but found he could not get a license. Friends had him do a little moonlighting plumbing for them but couldn't pay him much. So when a friend from the Navy wrote that he could get him a job on a construction contract, Barbour left for the West Coast. He did pretty well on construction jobs out there until the Korean War began. Then he was called back to active duty in the Navy.

"So, then I was back on the old job, keepin' the LST flushing systems workin'. I kept 'em goin' while we landed the boys for MacArthur's big end-around play at Inchon. And I kept 'em goin' when we took the boys off the beaches up

12

Grant's Place with cars parked in front.

north after the Chinese came into that thing. But, in between, I got a few good liberties in Japan to see how those Japanese babes was different than the Korean ones. Basically they's the same, I think; but don't ever tell *them* that!"

After the Korean War Grant received his discharge from the Navy and stayed on the West Coast for about ten more years. His account of his life during this time is somewhat unclear. He was apparently married and divorced at least twice. We have heard him mention the following jobs: construction work, "pearl diving," car washing, parking lot "jockey," cooking ("I'd got some better at it"), and bartending. Finally, "I bought me a one-fifth piece of a little bar and grill in West LA—just enough to make sure they couldn't fire me as bartender 'thout closing down the whole joint." He had this toehold in the business world for four years, until an emergency brought him back home to Spout Spring.

Grant's father and mother were still living in Sequoyah. They were quite old but had remained independent and self-sufficient, like most Spout Spring old people, until serious illness hit. "It was my father who was sick the worst," Grant told us. "Mama just sort of got porely, worryin' about him and workin' too hard takin' care of him. So finally I had to come back to help. Would you believe it, they neither one of them had gone to a doctor! I took Pop to one right away—to Doc Baxter. You know—the younger one. Well, it turned out he had cancer and was too far gone to do anything about it. So we knew he was dying, but we just had to sit and wait for him to do it. Took him a while; he was a pretty tough old guy. I had to sell out back in LA and get me a job, chef for the restaurant out to the Stony Point Motel, to meet expenses."

Grant's Place

After his father's death Grant surprised everybody by staying in Spout Spring. Even more surprisingly, he invested what money he had left in an apparently altruistic enterprise—a "teen-town club." He explained how this came about: "I seen these kids always hanging out on the street corners and it seemed like the idea of opening a place where they could come in an' play pool, eat snacks, and horse around—it just came to me and I went into it before stopping to think it over. I didn't expect to make any real money at it but I hoped to at least break even. Instead, I was payin' out for the privilege of bein' in business!"

Grant continued to work as a chef in the motel restaurant for over a year, hiring others to run the "Second Street Club." The venture was definitely a financial burden rather than a source of income, for that whole time. Then, in the summer of 1965, Grant decided to change the basic concept of the place. He began to see the need for an adult center in Spout Spring—and he figured that adults had more money to spend than teen-agers. So he applied for an on-premises beer-dispensing license.

The interesting thing is that Grant's application was successful. Undoubtedly this was a matter of good luck and good timing, combined with Grant's ability to rally financial backers. We have not been able to find out all the facts in the case, but three stand out as important. First, though the population and extent of the east side of Sequoyah had been expanding for some time, there were no taverns in the area. Second, nobody in the neighborhood raised any objections to the granting of the license. Third, Grant had influential friends, most of them White men, who lent him money for license fees, equipment, and supplies. An influential Black man, Spud Davison, also put in some money and helped make the White contacts. These contacts were probably helpful in getting the license granted. The money invested in this enterprise was well invested. Patronage quickly swung to the adult side, and the volume of business immediately increased to such an extent that Grant had to quit his restaurant job to devote his full time and energies to managing "Grant's Place."

The building that houses the tavern was formerly occupied by a Black lunch counter that served "soul food" to a limited Black clientele, before soul food was anything to fuss about. This business had not done very well. As Grant once pointed out to us: "The best cooks in Sequoyah live right down here in the neighborhood. So who needed a restaurant?"

The owner of the building was glad to have Grant move in with his original teen-town venture and was even happier to see it become a paying proposition after its transformation in 1965. He had rented it to Grant very cheaply in the beginning but felt obliged to raise the rent when the beer license went into effect.

The location of the tavern is a good one, on Second Street just east of Forbes Branch—one of the few level places of any extent in the little valley—and rather centrally located within the area of Black residence. The building is set back from the street about thirty feet, providing parking space for customers. Inside, there is a public front room that runs the entire width of the structure. Here Grant has installed a billiard table (originally part of the teen-town concept), a rough wooden bar, several table-bench booths, a soft-drink-dispensing machine, a cigarette-vending machine, and a juke-box type of record player. In back of the public front room, the space is divided up into smaller rooms. On the west end behind the bar are a kitchen and a refrigerated storeroom. On the east end is a slight anteroom, behind which there are men's and women's toilets. The floor space of the entire building is probably not over 625 square feet.

The Action at Grant's

The tavern is the most completely integrated institution in Sequoyah, and it is integrated on Black terms. Here Whites and Blacks meet and interact in a Black-owned establishment. It is currently an "in" place for OSU students, White and Black, as well as for local Blacks and Whites. None of these elements has "taken over" the place; it is not dominated by any clique of customers. Grant has a friendly but firmly positive personality, and he sets the tone of the place. It is down-to-earth and democratic, sometimes verging on rowdiness, but generally under the control of the proprietor. The local newspaper reports fights and arrests as occurring at Grant's about as frequently as in other taverns in Sequoyah. However, Grant claims these reports are usually inaccurate. He feels that there is a custom of reporting any disturbance in the neighborhood as occurring at Grant's Place. Quite possibly this results from rowdy persons who have been ejected from the tavern later coming to blows elsewhere but remembering that their fight developed out of an argument in the tavern.

By no means do all residents of the Spout Spring neighborhood frequent Grant's Place. In fact there is a strong church-oriented element that regards Grant's with some disapproval. Nevertheless, the tavern is the main focus of daily interaction in the community, on weekdays. Although the churches are more important to many people, church activities tend to be intermittent. Grant's, on the other hand, is open every day except Sunday, from 10 A.M. to midnight.

Grant's Place clearly fills an important need for Black men. Homes, schools, and churches have traditionally been centers of feminine influence; but Grant's Place, although it has women customers, is definitely male-dominated. Before the tavern was established, there had been no such center for Black men for at least ten years. There had once been an active Negro fraternal lodge and, for a brief period right after World War II, there was a "colored" veterans' organization. But both of these organizations are now extinct. What is now known as the Civic Club began in the 1920s as a men's business association; but today its members include a relatively small "elite" of public-spirited citizens, a majority of whom are women.

Grant's is a meeting place, a talking place. Men and women come and go throughout the day. Conversations go right on, with changing participants. Talk involves jobs, cars, women, politics, personalities, sports—and business deals. You can buy or sell things—cars, trucks, hogs, or washing machines—through encounters at Grant's.

Grant's is a sitting place. At all times of the day, men can be found sitting, relaxed, at booths inside the place or on benches outside. Usually they are also drinking, at least to the extent of having a can of beer in hand or near at hand, on table or bench. Sometimes they are not drinking at all, just there—sitting.

Grant's is a place of tension release. This function it shares with the three churches, whose values are variously opposed to the existence of this rival institution. Today few men get adequate emotional catharsis in the churches, though many women still do. Grant's provides a wide choice of means toward this end: talk, arguments, and even the fights that sometimes follow; dancing, singing, and shooting pool. All provide release from the tensions resulting from the restrictions imposed by society and custom.

The View

In the immediate neighborhood around Grant's, on both sides of Second Street are run-down houses—*substandard*, in the terminology of city planners. Some have, in fact, been abandoned and torn down, leaving empty spaces near the tavern. North and south of these houses facing the street are other houses on tributary mud alleys or "drives." Some of these houses are also "substandard" and deteriorated; others are "substandard" but better maintained. An ancient, two-story frame building on one of the off "drives" a half-block to the south is one of the two rooming houses in Spout Spring. It is probably the oldest structure in the neighborhood and among the oldest in Sequoyah—a farmhouse of a rather simple style built in the years following the Civil War.

There is a further view. Part of Birch Avenue, running along the side of East Mountain, is visible a half-block to the east. Up there are houses in greater

Grant's is a meeting place, a talking place.

variety, from deteriorated substandard to quite new. In general these houses are better kept than those near Grant's Place. The stream bed of Forbes Branch is visible both north and south of the Second Street bridge. Something of the charm of a spring-fed mountain stream still survives the litter of casually discarded urban culture.

Residents of Spout Spring can look beyond the immediate neighborhood, uphill to the west, north, or east, toward the political, commercial, and residential bastions of predominantly White Sequoyah. Most Black women and men move up out of the neighborhood, on foot or in cars or taxis, every weekday morning, to disperse among the hills and valleys of this other Sequoyah, where they earn their living. Much of their daily interaction is with White people—employers, fellow workers, and customers in the shops, garages, industries, and homes of the city. The Black children walk or ride up out of the neighborhood to attend schools with predominantly White student bodies and almost exclusively White teaching and administrative staffs. There are about 120 Black students, two Black teachers, and two Black practice teachers (from the OSU College of Education) in the Sequoyah public school system. Altogether there are about 5000 students and 250 teachers and administrators in the system (1968–1969 school year).

Most of these Black adults and children come back down into their little ghetto every day, late in the afternoon and early in the evening. Here their interactions are predominantly with other Blacks, in homes, yards, and streets, in churches, and in Grant's Place. A few individuals participate in civic or community organizations, which take them out of the neighborhood some evenings. A considerable number of people may go up during an evening to attend a popular film at the Osage Theater on Barrett Avenue while others go to the Plaza Theater on the Square or to a drive-in at the north end of the city. Moreover, during the day and in the evening too, some White people come down into Spout Spring on business or to visit friends or to drink beer at Grant's Place.

There is more integration between Blacks and Whites during daylight hours than during the night; there is more on weekdays than on weekends.

3

The Knight Family

OUR RECORDS INDICATE that the majority of families in the Sequoyah Black community fit the general United States pattern. This pattern is what sociologists and anthropologists call the nuclear-monogamous or nuclear-conjugal family, consisting of a stable married couple and their children. There are some important variations from this pattern, which we will discuss in Chapter 5. Here we set the stage for later discussions of economics and social organization with a description of the Knight family, a nuclear-conjugal family with six members.

The name Knight is fictitious (as are all personal names used in this book), and the personalities described are composites. We do not present the Knights as a completely typical or average family. Culture is too variable in the Spout Spring community to present a valid typical family. However, most personality traits and life circumstances we describe can be found in members of several families in Sequoyah or in their life experience.

The Knights live in a four-room house on the western slope rising out of the Valley. The house is plain and somewhat weather-beaten but well furnished, in a cluttered way. Bill and his wife, Rowena, have one bedroom; their daughter Mary Ann, uses the other. The three boys sleep in the living room. Bill drives a 1962 Ford pickup truck; Rowena drives a 1965 four-door Buick sedan.

Bill Knight

Bill Knight is forty-five years old, a middle-sized, powerfully built man with a gentle, stubborn face. The farm near Rush Hill on which Bill was born was owned by his grandfather. The Knight family has been in Lincoln County "since slavery days," having come in before the Civil War with a White family from Tennessee named Knight. After emancipation they were willed some land by their White namesakes at the time they took their name ("Knight's Jacob" be-

18

came Jacob Knight). Jacob Knight was Bill Knight's great grandfather. He passed this land down to Bill's grandfather, who divided it among his three sons in 1930 just before he died. All three sons lost their lands in mortgage foreclosures during the Depression of the 1930s. For about ten more years they hung on as renters or tenant farmers on the lands they formerly owned. But during those ten years agriculture faded out as a source of income or subsistence on the worn-out soils near Rush Hill. So members of the family began to move out, first to Sequoyah, where their children could get a better education than in the segregated three-month school in Rush Hill, and then on to other parts of the country.

Bill Knight's father was the last Knight to move his family out of Rush Hill. He established them in Sequoyah, then went alone to Tulsa, Oklahoma, where he got a job in a defense plant during the war. He kept his family in Sequoyah throughout this time, commuting back there on weekends as often as he could. After the war he returned in failing health, to Sequoyah, to die there in 1949. After that, Bill's mother and sisters moved to Los Angeles to live with Bill's older brother.

Bill Knight also left Sequoyah once; but he came back. As a boy he lived on the farm near Rush Hill and went to the little segregated school, which only "kept" for three months of the year. After he completed the third grade, his parents sent him to stay with an aunt in Sequoyah so that he could go to the nine-month Carver School. In a sense this move was the spearhead of the entire family's move into Sequoyah three years later. Bill did well in the Carver School and, after he completed all of its grades, he went to Tulsa to stay with his father and to begin high school. He also worked, and the work interfered with his schooling. Discouraged, he enlisted in the Navy. He served in the Pacific theater during the last year of World War II and for two years after the war; he advanced to the rating of Motor Machinist's Mate, Second Class. After his discharge from the Navy, he settled in the Los Angeles area, first living with his brother, later setting up his own household. While working at an aircraft plant in Santa Monica, he met Sheila Carter, a Sequoyah girl who had come out to Los Angeles to visit relatives, liked it there, and got a job. Bill and Sheila became engaged and soon married.

After his marriage Bill continued to work and put part of his savings into tuition for Sheila at a beauticians' school. During this period their first child, a son, was born. After completing her training as a beautician, Sheila obtained steady work as a beauty operator, but Bill lost his job at the aircraft plant. Both were without steady work during Sheila's pregnancy with their daughter. After that she did not want more children, as she felt her job was the mainstay of the family. Bill went through a trying time during which he was often unemployed or, for very short periods, working at odd jobs. Much of the time he took care of the children and did tasks in the home. Sheila's job did, in fact, become the main source of income for the family, and Sheila became increasingly self-assertive. She "came by this naturally"; her family has a tradition in Sequoyah for female efficiency and self-sufficiency.

Though Bill worked willingly around the house when not working at a job, he did not take easily to the role of subordinate husband-father. It was not a role that had been acceptable in the Knight family. His own father had made considerable sacrifices of health and time with his family in order to maintain the breadwinner role during the war. Only after the war, when his health was failing, had the elder Knight been relatively less productive of income than his wife.

Early in the 1950s, during Sheila's annual vacation, Bill, Sheila, and their two children paid a brief visit to Sequoyah. They stayed with her sisters in their home in the Spout Spring neighborhood. The sisters urged Bill and Sheila to remain permanently in Sequoyah. Bill was strongly attracted to the idea; Sheila was not. So they returned to Los Angeles. After a series of increasingly violent disagreements, they had a climactic quarrel, in which Sheila taunted Bill with his inability to provide income. She especially asserted her right to have the dominant role in disciplining the children. Bill felt that she was inconsistent and sometimes extremely harsh toward the children. His own treatment of the children, in his opinion, had been gentler and more consistent.

After the quarrel he borrowed bus fare from friends and returned to Sequoyah. When he arrived there, he stayed for a while with Sheila's sisters, who tried to patch up the differences between him and Sheila. Eventually, however, Sheila obtained a divorce.

Bill views the Los Angeles interlude in his life with a peculiar combination of bitterness and objectivity. "Sheila's a good woman, when she isn't on a hateful streak. She just come on too strong when she began makin' money. I wasn't used to that and wasn't about to try to be. Also, she fits in—in L.A. I don't. She could get a good job—and I couldn't. There was ways I could have made money that you might not exactly call legal. I had several chances. Even tried it once; but I didn't like it. I never knew whether Sheila tho't I should have done that stuff or not. But that's not my way of doin'—of makin' money. I don't respect it and I couldn't be any good at it. My Daddy wouldn't have respected that kind of thing nor my Mother wouldn't've. But that's all there was for me there, at least then. Reason I come back here, I figured I could always get some kind of honest work here, if I wanted it bad enough."

As a matter of fact, after Bill came back to Sequoyah, he was rather disappointed by the kind of work that was available. "Most of the men were working up around the campus, at that time. Mostly, they made chicken-feed wages. You could be a porter or a houseboy or maybe cook. Two things I don't like to be called are 'boy' and 'cat.' But plenty of White people have called me 'boy' and plenty of colored people have called me 'cat.' I'm not a 'boy' any more and I never was what they mean when they say 'cat'—at least not much. But you have to know how to take things folks say, if that's the way they talk. Lots of those kids up in the frat houses and sorority houses were mean and spoiled; but most of 'em were pretty decent. They probably thought it was o.k. to to say 'boy' to a colored man, if he was working for them. They had heard their daddies and their mamas say that all their lives. But it was hard taking that and the kind of money that went with it, for the work up there. Especially after coming back from L.A. talking big about what kind of work I would do. Sometimes I figured I was a fool for turning my back on good easy money out there for small change back here."

As time went by, Bill found that he could supplement his small wages at the fraternities and sororities by doing extra work or extra favors for individuals or groups. The extra favors often included activities that were illegal, such as selling whiskey on Sundays. Bill also made money out of a kind of concession for the soft-drink machine in one fraternity where he worked. Despite these additions to his income, he was glad when jobs began to open up for Blacks in the automotive sales and service business around Sequoyah. "I was always pretty good with motors. I've always kept my own cars running. So when Joe Rush asked me to work for him at his used-car place, and offered me a pretty decent kind of pay, for then, I was glad to move out to that. But, you know, at first I actually made less than I was making up on the Hill with my fraternity job and the soft-drink machine."

Bill has always done extra work outside his main job. These are moonlighting jobs; cleaning offices in the evening, yard work, and other odd jobs. In 1955 Bill married again and began having more children to feed and clothe.

Bill's work in the automative-service field began at an unskilled level and, even today, is hard to pinpoint on a scale of status or skill. Much of his work involves cleaning up cars on a used-car lot, charging batteries, and delivering or picking up cars. Beyond that he works at fixing cars traded in to the lot. This can include anything from matching a hubcap to repairing a carburetor. The Black men of Sequoyah who work for garages, new- and used-car dealers, or in other automotive enterprises share a common occupational subculture of know-how and expertise. Among these men there is a subtle hierarchy of prestige, based as much on acknowledged skills as on income. Bill Knight does not rate at the top of this hierarchy on a par with the Dawson brothers. On the other hand, he rates considerably more respect than that accorded certain young men who only sweep floors, deliver cars, and change an occasional tire. Bill really spans all levels of skills, or most of them; he is a kind man of all work for Joe Rush. He likes Rush, but not without some reservations. For instance, he feels that he is not paid what he is worth and that Rush does not fully appreciate how nearly indispensable he has become to the business.

"Joe and I knew each other as boys," he points out. "We growed up together in the west end of the county. In fact, you could say we're kind of cousins. That's one reason he give me a job in the first place, when he bought up this business. At least, that's what he told me once, when we was drinkin' in his office one cold winter evening. You see, we both know that one of his great-grand-daddies was my mama's grand-daddy. Trouble is, he comes on like it's a big favor, him having me work for him. It *was* when he first hired me. Now, though, I figure I'm the one's doin' the favor. I do most of the mechanical work around the lot, and he'd have to pay plenty to get it done, otherwise. Also, I could go to work several other places, if I wanted, and get more money than what Joe pays me. But I will say he's easy to work for. He knows I know what's to be done, without him always ridin' herd on me. I like that part of it."

Rowena Knight

Rowena Knight is thirty-five years old. She and Bill have been married for thirteen years and have four children: Bill Jr., age twelve; Joe-Jack, ten; Mary Ann, nine; and Bobby, seven. Rowena was twenty-two years old when she married Bill. She grew up in Sequoyah and has spent most of her life there, except for the years 1951 to 1954 during high school when she lived with an aunt in Kansas City, Missouri. (The Sequoyah High School was one of the first in the state of Ozarka to integrate, but it did not do so until 1954.)

Rowena's family managed to send her to Pine Bluff, Arkansas, for one year at the AM&N Negro college there. Then she had to return to Sequoyah to help her family financially. She returned to Sequoyah disappointed but willing to help in any way possible. At first she worked as a baby-sitter and at various day-work cleaning jobs until she met and married Bill Knight. Then, as the children arrived, she would take off work long enough to get each baby past the infant stage, but inevitably had to find work again somewhere to help out with the rising costs of living for a growing family. Later, after her youngest reached nursery-school age and the three older children were in grade school, she got her present job, working five days a week as a housekeeper, cook, and nursemaid for a university teacher's family.

To compensate for their inability to be full-time parents, Rowena and Bill borrowed money a few years ago to pay tuition and board for Bobby in a Catholic nursery-kindergarten (though they are Baptists). They then had to live very frugally for a while to pay off the loan and meet other expenses at the same time. Rowena feels, "It was worth it because they treated the baby good and gave him good food and taught him manners and things he would need to know when he started in to school." They did not send Bobby to the COA-sponsored Sequoyah Day Care Center, as they were "above income," according to the EOA poverty-defining guidelines.

Many men and women in the Sequoyah Black community are above average in physical attractiveness, by both White and Black standards. Such good looks tend to be family characteristics. Rowena would be able to compete with attractive women in any society if she were comparably dressed. She is also a shrewd and canny manager of both her own household and that of her employer. She has the strong character and comfortable personality shared by most of the Black women of Sequoyah, qualities attained through many years of working for Whites in a White-dominated society. Rowena and others like her have arrived at a kind of compatibility with White employers, a compatibility in which White dominance and Black subordination have been tempered by mutual respect and interdependence. Like Bill, Rowena recognizes the efforts needed to get and keep a job in any place. Like him, she also prefers to make the struggle in an environment of comparative peace, in a community where she has the companionship and moral support of long-time friends and relatives.

In spite of a demanding schedule of work and home duties, Rowena makes a real effort to contribute some time to church, community, and civil rights when she feels they are worthwhile. She says, "I do what I can, *when* I can. But sometimes it's hard to decide which is more important—my people, my husband, or just paying the bills. But I do hate to go to a meeting and sit there watching them doing nothing but talk and 'spin their wheels.'"

While accepting the limitations of employment for herself and Bill, Rowena hopes and works for better education for her children, believing that this will consequently bring better jobs and more affluent living conditions for them. She and Bill see integration of the schools in Sequoyah (and elsewhere) as an eventual answer to several problems and feel that Blacks as a whole will profit from this change. At the same time they are a little sad that their own children must be the ones to face so many new adjustment problems connected with old prejudices involving both Blacks and Whites.

The Knight Children

Bill Knight, Jr., pitches for a Little League baseball team. He is one of three Black boys on that team. Bill, Sr., and another Black father alternate as coaches for the team, adjusting their moonlighting work schedules to make this possible. The other coaches are fathers of some of the White boys on the team. The manager is a young White man who is a physical education major at OSU. The other coaches get along well with Bill, Sr., and they treat Bill, Jr., fairly. This is easy, as the boy is one of the two best players on the team. The other is a White boy and the only White boy on the team whom Bill, Jr., can't get along with. "He can't help it, I guess. That other boy's a red-neck type, always actin' mean and sayin' bad things to the colored kids. My son don't take that," explained Bill, Sr.

Bill, Jr., takes his baseball very seriously, and so does his father. They have some hopes that he will go on to play for Sequoyah High School and possibly in college. Somewhere along the way they dream that he will impress a major league scout and get a bonus contract. Young Bill's physical development does give promise that this dream may be realistic. He is a lean, intense kid, with a whiplash arm, quick reflexes, and serious dedication to baseball. He is already almost as tall as his father and will undoubtedly exceed him in height eventually. In addition to his pitching talents, Bill, Jr., is a good batter and a capable outfielder. But he feels that, in the long run, pitching offers him the best future. His father agrees. "They's never enough good pitchers," he points out. "Billy Junior's going to be good; he got a strong arm and he's been taught right how to use it but not to abuse it. That what a pitcher's got to know."

Bill, Sr., is especially concerned to keep close to Bill, Jr., and to the other children, because he fears losing contact with them in the teen years. "I don't want him to get like some of these young-'uns are, talkin' mean and doin' nothin' but get into trouble. One reason I come back here was to get away from that big city kind of way of talkin' and livin'. Now that stuff is spreading all over and we got it right here too, some. I blame folks for not watchin' their kids an' teachin' them right. Billy Junior's goin' t' school and he's goin' to learn to stand up for his-self. But he's not goin' down into the gutter t' do it."

Bill, Jr., is somewhat fascinated by the images of Black militancy that Sequoyah youngsters now see on TV and that are reflected in the behavior of some Black teen-agers. He sees baseball as his own route to the future; but he thinks that Black pride and Black toughness are needed for most young people. He feels that his father sees things in an old-fashioned way—that maybe he doesn't really understand what's going on in the world. He respects the rebellious mood of the Black teen-agers and says that he may join them if he doesn't get fair breaks in sports. Most Black youngsters in Sequoyah feel that they are not treated fairly in the schools and that this includes biased treatment of athletes. They especially point out that Black athletes do not make the teams at OSU, and most of them feel that the university faculty people look down on them.

Young Joe-Jack Knight is impressed when his older brother talks about Black militancy, but he tries not to show it. He says, "He jus' tryin' t' act big when he talks that way." Joe-Jack admires Bill, Jr., as an athlete and is somewhat jealous of his prowess. Joe-Jack plays baseball too, on another team. But he is just an average player, not a star. In other ways he has tended to remain in the shadow of his older brother. He is smaller and more easy-going, lacking his brother's tense drive and determination. He plays ball for the fun of it, enjoys his hits and other successes, but readily forgives himself his strikeouts and fielding errors.

Bill, Sr., and Joe-Jack have a different kind of relationship than the father has with Bill, Jr. It is a kind of joking, happy-go-lucky fondness, in which there is less ambitious concern for the future. Bill, Sr., wants Joe-Jack to get educated and to get a good job; but all this seems far off, part of a generalized future, although Joe-Jack is only a scant two years younger than Bill, Jr. When the family goes on a fishing and picnic outing at Lost Bridge on a summer week-end, Bill, Sr., shares his fishing lore with both boys. But somehow it is Joe-Jack who understands and responds best and to whom Bill, Sr., in turn responds with fun and good fellowship.

Mary Ann Knight feels that she has been wronged because she has no sisters to back her up against so many boys. She has a certain awe of her oldest brother; but she regards her other brothers as rivals and nuisances: Joe-Jack because he pesters her; little Bobby because she is supposed to be responsible for him a good part of her free time. She is also fiercely jealous that her father now spends so much of his spare time with the boys and so little with her. It used to be different. Mary Ann was sick a lot when she was younger. Because of an asthmatic condition she had to delay starting school for a whole year. During that year, and during all of her younger "sickly" years, Bill, Sr., was much concerned about her and devoted all the time he could spare to playing with her or just holding her. Then it was the boys who felt neglected and jealous.

Bobby is still referred to as "the baby," which makes him mildly indignant. Nevertheless, he gladly takes advantage of the special privileges that his overextended infant status entails. Because the Knights are now somewhat better off than they were when the other children were little, Bobby has probably been more indulged than the others.

The Knight children fight and scream about the house a good deal. It is a crowded house, and they get into each other's way a lot. Sometimes this aggravates either Bill or Rowena beyond endurance, and they try to shout the children down to achieve a semblance of quiet. In this they were not usually very successful until Bill recently bought a color TV set. This has calmed things down somewhat, and the children seem to take up less space while they are watching the shows.

In school most of the children do fairly well. Bill, Jr., is at present the best student, despite his athletic preoccupations. Joe-Jack is the poorest, so far as grades are concerned. Yet he seems the most curious about things he doesn't know and, when he gets really interested, spends more time reading than the others.

Mary Ann does well enough but is plagued and worried by the bullying of a bigger girl at school. Vivian is a Black child, too, but she was born in Chicago, where she lived until a year ago. She came to Sequoyah with her mother (a native of Sequoyah) and three other children after the mother's marriage broke up. Vivian is poorer and more aggressive than most of the other Black children, and she tries to dominate them. As the target for her resentment, she has singled out Mary Ann.

One day when Mary Ann was walking home from school, Vivian suddenly attacked her. Mary Ann took refuge in the city library building, where she recognized a White woman as a friend of her mother and ran up to her to ask for help. The White woman talked with both Mary Ann and her tormentor, trying unsuccessfully to arrange a truce. Because Vivian remained definitely belligerent, and Mary Ann became more and more terrified, the White woman finally drove Mary Ann home. She told Rowena about the problem. Rowena could only say, "I know who she is, and it's no use my talking with that girl's mother. She won't do anything about it. She's got pretty tough herself, since she's been gone from here, and I'd rather not have any more to do with her than I have to. Her kids are left on their own most of the time; so they do just about whatever they want to and get by with it."

Rowena admitted that "Mary Ann has been raised in a different way and she hasn't never run into that kind of kid before."

Rowena loves all her children; but Mary Ann is her only daughter, which makes her special. Rowena makes an effort to dress her better than the other children—and this may be one cause for Vivian's hostility. Vivian's clothing is obviously old and ill-fitting, and she is generally neglected in appearance. Although she says she is eleven years old, she looks older in the face and is "wiry-thin." In comparison Mary Ann has a soft, healthy roundness. While Mary Ann is ready and willing to forgive and forget, even to try to be friends with the girl, Vivian apparently doesn't know how to back down gracefully. She seems actually to take a certain satisfaction in being the aggressor. Vivian's parting words to the White lady who took Mary Ann home from the library were, "I'll maybe not get her today; but I'll get her some other day. I'll get her no matter if I have to try every day. She said somethin' bad about me and I'm goin' to get her."

Bill and Rowena

Bill Knight first met Rowena at the Carter house shortly after he came back from Los Angeles. Rowena was a good friend of the Carter sisters and used to drop in to visit with them evenings or weekends. She had just come back from the college at Pine Bluff and was trying to get started earning money. The Carter sisters had always been good friends of her family, and they tried to help the young girl adjust to coming back from college to take up the traditional domestic work of Sequoyah Black women.

Bill, who was then staying with the Carter sisters until he could get himself established back in Sequoyah, saw Rowena as an attractive young girl who seemed rather naïve about the ways of the world. His more serious interest in her came later, after he had begun to make a little money and had rented a room in the local rooming house. He bought an old car and began dating several girls casually, "playing the field." He saw Rowena in church several times and eventually asked her out. She refused twice, backed out of a date once, and finally began going out with him. When he had a date with another girl, she turned him down five times in one month and only agreed to go out with him again if he'd stop going with anyone else. By this time his divorce became final in California, and Bill and Rowena became engaged. Soon afterward they married and moved into their present home, which Rowena had recently inherited from an aunt.

The thirteen years of their marriage have been full of crises—most of them financial, some emotional. The financial crises have been met with close cooperation. The emotional crises have been sudden outbursts interrupting the otherwise smooth teamwork of the two. Bill is probably more patient with Rowena, most of the time, than he ever was with his first wife. But he has stubborn, offbeat moods, usually aggravated by drinking, when Rowena can't understand him and fears that he is slipping away from her. Rowena is a strong personality but more subtle and feminine than Sheila. She has great patience too—most of the time. In her years of domestic work and marriage, she has become an excellent cook and housekeeper, as well as a good manager. At times she becomes suddenly jealous of Sheila, or of other women. Generally Rowena's jealousy has no basis in fact, and certainly there is none in Sheila's case. Bill has seen Sheila only twice, and briefly, since he left Los Angeles.

Bill and Rowena have a pretty good thing going sexually, in addition to their general compatability in economic and family relationships. This has kept them both from having any serious outside adventures. Yet each, prizing the other so highly as a sexual partner, feels that the other must be irresistible to all others. Thus, they occasionally become jealous of imagined suitors. It is true that both do have opportunities for extramarital dalliance but they don't take advantage of them. They consider the existence of opportunities stimulating but unimportant.

During the period when Bill was bootlegging for students at OSU, Rowena gave him a hard time about it. She once nearly left him because he failed to stop after promising that he would. There were also two occasions when Bill got drunk and pushed her around and slapped her. Both times he had become depressed about financial problems and took exception to "frivolous" expenditures she made (with money she had earned). For several years his drinking was potentially a really serious problem. But her threat to leave him permanently and take the children if he got drunk again has had its effect. He has not been really drunk for several years. Two or three times a week, he stops off at Grant's Place for a few beers on the way home from work. About once a month he drinks a pint of Jack Daniels at home on a weekend. Rowena does not drink.

Their jealousy, too, has slacked off in recent years, and they both feel more secure about their marriage. Rowena's sense of security increased noticeably after Bill's two children by his first wife spent three weeks with them during the summer of 1967. After years of separation from the children, Bill had looked forward to this visit with both delight and trepidation. Rowena had frankly dreaded it, but as it turned out, the visit was pleasant, even placid and rather dull, for all concerned. The former close relationship of a young man with two babies had little resemblance to the friendly but constrained encounter of a mature man with two respectful but somewhat "hip" teen-agers. After some initial shyness, the visit went smoothly. Rowena actually got closer to Bill's daughter than Bill did himself. He was rather relieved when the children left, though he looks forward to some unspecified future encounter.

Despite inflation the Knight's current prosperity seems secure—if they can both keep working. But from years of too much work and too little care for their health, Bill and Rowena have been subject to ailments lately. And they have practically no savings. Although they own the house they live in, it is getting old and needs constant repairs. Groceries, payments on the TV, upkeep of the car, clothing and medical needs for a family of six—all these keep them working hard to make ends meet. A serious disabling illness for either Bill or Rowena could be a major disaster, affecting present comfort and future prospects for the children and for themselves. Each fears for the other and for the damage the disability of either could bring. Both hope that their health will hold up at least until the youngest child is grown and on his own in the world.

4

Making a Living

MOST BLACK ADULTS IN SEQUOYAH are wage-earners in service occupations of an unskilled or semiskilled type. A majority of the men do clean-up work of various kinds—or work for automotive sales or service companies in jobs that combine clean-up work with such semiskilled mechanical work as tire-changing or lubrication. Most women are employed in domestic jobs. In addition to the unskilled or semiskilled majority, there are some skilled workers and a small number of persons who can be classified as managers, professionals, or proprietors. This last category—"professional-managerial-proprietary"—includes only fifteen persons in a work force of over two hundred. The small size of the Black population is a relevant factor here. There are not enough Black people in Sequoyah to support many businessmen or professionals.

There is an implicit barrier dividing jobs that have been traditionally considered Negro jobs from other occupations. Thus, until recently, there has been little competition between Blacks and Whites for jobs. Whites held certain jobs; Negroes held certain other jobs. But the distinction, maintained by custom and hiring practices, has never been absolutely rigid. There have always been exceptions —special cases—and there have been quiet changes in definition of White and Negro jobs in the past. So our statements must be read with these qualifications in mind.

Negro women have practically dominated domestic employment jobs in Sequoyah—as day-work housecleaners, housekeepers, cooks, maids, nursemaids for children, or various combinations of these specialized tasks. But a rather interesting dichotomy has prevailed with respect to men's clean-up work. Negroes could work as dishwashers, porters, houseboys, yardmen, and janitors in homes, offices, garages, and private businesses. In addition, they had a monopoly on jobs of these types in fraternities and sororities on or near the OSU campus. But White men dominate maintenance or clean-up jobs with public agencies. For instance, all employees of the maintenance crew at OSU are White. All employees of the city Sanitation Department (garbage collectors, etc.) are White, as are all other

28

city and county employees at this and most other levels. This situation, reflects a shift in job definition that took place some forty years ago. We know, for instance that some Negroes worked for the university in maintenance jobs during the early decades of the present century. Garbage collection within the city was once a private function unofficially assigned to Negro men, who performed the service free in order to use the edible portions of the garbage to feed hogs they raised on the outskirts of town. During the depression of the 1930s, Whites apparently moved into such jobs with public agencies.

Blacks have been barred traditionally from most semiskilled and skilled jobs. However, traditional exceptions to this rule involved certain aspects of food preparation or food handling. Cooks, grocery-store stockmen, and slaughterhouse butchers could be Negroes. But, with only occasional exceptions, no Negroes held jobs as waiters or waitresses, grocery clerks, or retail butchers—except in businesses catering exclusively or largely to Blacks. At present there are no such establishments in Sequoyah. This customary situation has been changing very gradually ever since World War II; during the past decade change has accelerated. Today the job barrier has been successfully penetrated by a fair number of Black people. Our data on jobs contain empirical evidence of the gains made. (A later section of this chapter treats this breakthrough in some detail.)

Jobs

According to our records, there are 250 adult Negroes in Sequoyah. The effective work force is considerably smaller, as there are forty-two persons not actively on the job market. These include eight housewives not seeking work, twenty-one persons who are too old to work or are physically incapacitated, and thirteen students in colleges or universities. Of the remaining 208 persons, two hundred are working and eight—six men and two women—are seeking jobs. These figures, which refer to September 1968, do not include teen-agers who hold temporary summer jobs or work part-time during the school year. High school graduates and dropouts are included, however.

We divided the jobs held by Sequoyah Black people into four main categories, based on functional analysis of the work involved, as revealed to us in interviews. These four categories are: Unskilled; Semiskilled; Skilled; and Professional-Managerial-Proprietary (referred to as "Prof-Man-Prop" in our tables). Men and women appear in these categories as follows:

MEN		WOMEN
54	Unskilled	72
29*	Semiskilled	14
11	Skilled	5
9	Prof-Man-Prop	6
103		97

* Includes 10 men in the armed forces.

Unskilled jobs for men include maintenance and clean-up jobs of various kinds; for women, domestic day work and other nonspecialized domestic jobs. These are all traditional Negro jobs in Sequoyah.

Semiskilled jobs for men include tire recappers, stockmen in groceries and pharmacies, slaughterhouse butchers, and auto lubrication workers. Women's jobs in this category include cooks and housekeepers—domestic workers with some degrees of responsibility and skill. Most of the men's jobs in this category are relatively new and represent job breakthroughs; but most of the women's jobs are traditional Negro jobs.

Men's jobs in the skilled category of work include auto body-and-fender workers, bakers, construction craft workers, a machinist, a heavy-duty truck driver, a mechanic, and an electrician. Women's jobs in this category include office workers and telephone company operators. The men's jobs are at least relatively new, except for the bakers. The women's jobs are all very new, representing breakthroughs achieved only within the past two years.

The men's professional-managerial-proprietary category includes five small businessmen, three professionals, and one manager. Five of the women classified in this category are professionals or semiprofessionals. The sixth is a proprietor. Most of the people in this category occupy traditional Negro roles, as they are defined in Sequoyah. The few exceptions can be viewed as cases of tokenism. The really significant changes in the job situation for Sequoyah Blacks have for the most part involved the opening up of new opportunities in the semiskilled and skilled categories.

Professionals, Manager, and Proprietors

A brief consideration of the individual occupations in this category illustrates the relatively superficial character of most of them, from the point of view of changes in occupational opportunities.

Three of the five businessmen on our list operate shoeshine stands. In each case, the operator owns the stand and the equipment he uses but has his stand set up in a White-owned barber shop. All clients are Whites. The average customer in these barber shops would hardly think of these shoeshine stands as businesses. Yet there is a distinction between these operations and the marginal jobs some Negroes have held as shoeshine boys in barber shops or hotels, where the stands and equipment belonged to the larger establishment.

A fourth businessman is the barber of the Black community. His shop is in his home. There are no Black barbers cutting White men's hair in Sequoyah; nor do White barbers cut Black men's hair. According to the Black barber, there are different technical problems involved in cutting White men's hair, and he prefers not to do it. In any case the existence of a distinctively Black barber shop is a traditional aspect of the "business world" in Sequoyah.

The fifth businessman on our list is Grant Barbour, the tavern owner. He represents a new business type for Sequoyah Blacks (at least on a legal basis). Black-run taverns with predominantly Black patronage are, of course, quite traditional in larger Black communities. But the strongly biracial character of Grant's Place is a new thing in Sequoyah; it would probably be regarded as unusual anywhere in the United States, but certainly in the South.

Two of the professionals on our list are pastors. One is Reverend L. J. Allen, the Methodist minister. The other is Brother Graham Shaw, the Church of Christ preacher. The Baptist church recently lost its preacher, who was "called" to a church in another state. Reverend Allen and Brother Shaw are actually retired men living on pensions from secular jobs. In a sense they are professionals by courtesy rather than by training—although each has spent a good deal of time in preparing himself for his religious work. Reverend Allen is said to receive $35 for each sermon delivered. According to our information, Brother Shaw receives no pay at all.

The third professional on our list in Ralph Evans, former principal of Carver School, who now teaches physical education in junior high school. The shift from the traditional role of Negro teacher in a segregated school to the new role of Black teacher in an integrated school is certainly significant. However, the demotion in job status is characteristic of what has happened to many Black school administrators throughout the South during the past ten years. There is certainly tokenism here. The retention of Mr. Evans in the school system is useful as evidence that the teaching staff is integrated, but it is extremely unlikely that he will ever again become a school principal in the Sequoyah system.

The most significant new job in the professional category is held by Joe Carter, who is Neighborhood Center Director in Sequoyah for the Lincoln County Community Outreach Agency. Even this is, in a sense, a case of tokenism. The local antipoverty agency, being federally funded, *must* establish itself as an integrated institution. However, the potentiality of this job goes beyond tokenism. Joe Carter is a significant and dynamic force in the administration of the COA. His influence goes far beyond the limits of his job designation. Because he has this job, he has become an important leader in the Black community. But his influence extends into the White community as well.

Two of the six women in the professional-managerial-proprietary category also work for the COA. One is Mrs. Daphne Newton, a practical nurse. The other is Mrs. Lucy Mae Norman, assistant director of the Head-Start program in Sequoyah. Mrs. Norman was formerly a teacher in the segregated Carver School. Mrs. Mary Winters, a professional social worker and recent OSU graduate, works for a federal job-training program closely associated with the COA, though separately funded. Two more women, Mrs. Doris Reed and Miss Stella Stark, work as trainees in a practical-nursing program.

The women listed in this category represent more significant changes in occupational status than do the men. There is probably some tokenism, but what is important is the need to find and train qualified people in fields where there are serious shortages of personnel. As far as we can ascertain, the competence of these Black women is at least on a par with that of White women of comparable experience in their respective jobs.

The one proprietor on our list of women represents a traditional occupational activity. Mrs. Selma Welty runs a rooming house in the Spout Spring neighborhood. It is a small establishment, with only one or two permanent roomers; other rooms are available for transients. Formerly Mrs. Welty also ran a small grocery store, but she closed that business over ten years ago and is regarded as partially retired.

Part-Time Businesses

The preceding section indicates that at least some of the persons in the Professional-Managerial-Proprietary are not earning their full living from their work in this category. We included Mrs. Welty and the preachers in this category only because they are not regularly working at any other kind of job and are still too active to be regarded as fully retired. If part-time moonlighting by persons earning substantial portions of their incomes from regular daytime jobs were counted, the list of persons in the category would have to be expanded by about 50 percent. Several men and women run fairly profitable small business operations on the side.

Perhaps the outstanding moonlighter is Paul Hull, a skilled carpenter who works during the daytime for a White contractor. After hours he does a good deal of contracting on his own and may well soon strike out independently on a full-time basis. Several men have small evening businesses involving contracts to clean up stores and offices. They have pickup trucks or panel trucks especially rigged to carry cleaning equipment. Several women work evenings or weekends in their homes as hair stylists and beauticians, though none of them works at this full-time. There is at least one bootlegger (whose main business is done on Sundays), an electrician, and a musician who plays drums in a jazz combo on weekends.

The part-time business or occupation was once the principal way of by-passing the job barrier. By moonlighting, several enterprising Black men and women earned higher incomes than would otherwise have been possible, but at the cost of much weariness and loss of time with their families. Perhaps the outstanding example is Charles "Spud" Davison, an elderly man now officially retired. For many years he worked as a stockman and deliveryman for a drugstore but probably made more money as a salesman, moneylender, and "promoter" than at his regular job. Today he owns houses and real estate and has investments in several enterprises in Sequoyah and elsewhere. He is probably the wealthiest Black man in Sequoyah.

Men, Women, and the Job Barrier

Sequoyah Blacks—especially the men—have a markedly conservative attitude concerning jobs. Many adults, particularly middle-aged and elderly adults, seem to accept the traditional definitions concerning jobs appropriate for Negroes. Younger people and women seem less likely to accept the traditional definition. The job barrier is naturally accepted more completely among people who have grown up with it and have seen it questioned only recently. Yet the barrier has been penetrated, and by these same apparently conservative people. Very quietly and very slowly this penetration has been going on for at least twenty years. The pace is increasing. Some recent breakthroughs by women have been quite spectacular. But in the over-all picture there have been more job breakthroughs by Black men than by Black women. This becomes clear when we compare our 1968 job data with data from the period before World War II.

The Sequoyah city directory of 1935 gives job data on ninety-four Negro men and thirty-six Negro women. (We suspect that these data are more nearly complete for men than for women.) A classification of the jobs in terms of our job-skill categories shows the following distribution:

MEN		WOMEN
70	Unskilled	12
10	Semiskilled	23
5	Skilled	0
6	Prof-Man-Prop	1
91*		36

* 3 men are listed as retired.

The striking contrast between these figures and those for 1968 is in the men's job-skill categories. In 1935 nearly 75 percent of the men's jobs were in the unskilled category, as compared to 53.4 percent in 1968. In 1935 12 percent of the men's jobs were semiskilled; in 1968 the figure is 28.2 percent. In 1935 4.4 percent of the men's jobs were skilled; in 1968 the figure is 10.7 percent. In the 1935 information, 6.4 percent of the men were in the professional-managerial-proprietary category; in 1968 this had risen slightly, to 8.7 percent.

Although the data on women's jobs for 1935 are probably incomplete, they suggest that women's jobs were better in 1935 than in 1968. This is an inference from the fact that over 63 percent of the women's jobs were in the semiskilled category and only 33 percent were in the unskilled category. This compares with a 1968 picture that more than reverses the percentages: less than 15 percent semiskilled and over 74 percent unskilled. Although unskilled women's jobs may have been seriously underreported in 1935, the semiskilled jobs of 1935 were nevertheless more numerous than in 1968. The work involved was mostly in jobs as cooks and housekeepers. Probably fewer White families now maintain establishments requiring fully specialized cooks or housekeepers.

A more detailed look at the actual jobs reveals the general trend of change, especially in men's work. Men's unskilled jobs in 1935 included janitors, porters, houseboys, and laborers—all jobs found in the unskilled category today. Semiskilled jobs included: a fairgrounds attendant, a cleaner at a laundry, a gardener, and several cooks. In 1968 there is no fairgrounds attendant, but all the other jobs can be matched in the current list. But, in addition, the 1968 jobs include tire recappers, wholesale butchers, and auto lubrication workers, as well as stockmen in groceries and pharmacies. Men's skilled jobs in 1935 included a theater fireman and three farmers. These are gone from the 1968 list, but that list includes many skilled jobs not present in 1968: auto body-and-fender workers, bakers, craft workers in construction, a mechanic, a machinist, a long-distance truck driver, and an electrician. The professional-managerial-proprietary category of 1935 included a contractor, a teacher, two shoeshine parlor operators, and two pastors. All of these are still present on a full-time or part-time basis. But, in addition, the 1968 list includes a tavern proprietor, a barber (probably a sideline in 1935), and the COA Center director.

All women's jobs present in 1935 are present in 1968, except laundress. Jobs present in 1968 but absent in our brief 1935 list include office workers, telephone operators, the Head-Start assistant director, the social worker, the COA practical nurse, and the practical-nursing trainees.

Although the women's gains in the last category represent some rather dramatic job breakthroughs, the comparative data on men's jobs are quantitatively more impressive. The whole concept of what constitutes an appropriate job for a Black man has shifted upward. The generation that has achieved this unspectacular but solid change consists of men who were children or adolescents in 1935. Between 1940 and 1945 many men of this generation went into the armed forces. Those who came back had altered self-concepts, self-concepts that hardly seem dramatic today. They aspired to better jobs, better incomes, and a more adequate fulfillment of the masculine role. Only some of the men have fully succeeded in attaining these goals, and it has taken them a long time. Most of them are not fully aware of what they have achieved, and some are either cynical or resigned to what seems a basically static situation. They are not particularly impressed, for instance, by recent, rather sudden occupational breakthroughs, which they interpret as tokenism, failing to realize, perhaps, that what looks like tokenism may actually be the logical next steps in a process they began.

Thus we are faced with an apparent contradiction. Women are more change-oriented than men; yet, in terms of jobs, the men have actually been effecting more changes than the women. Actually there is no real contradiction. Many Black women in Sequoyah have very high aspirations with respect to economic change for *all* Blacks, and especially for their children and for their men, as well as for themselves. The men have lower but more immediate aspirations, mainly toward pay raises within their current job categories. They also seek to exploit small-scale breakthroughs to slightly higher job categories, which they may attain without too much "fuss."

Viewed in long-term perspective, however, some of the job mobility of men has really been very considerable. This is well exemplified in the careers of two leading pioneers of the job breakthrough into automotive work—the Dawson brothers, Dan and Joe. Both saw overseas service and received mechanical training in the armed forces during World War II. Dan ended up as a motor machinist's mate, first class, in the Navy. Joe got as far as corporal a couple of times while driving Army supply trucks in France. (Both times he got "busted" back down to PFC for "sassing" White superiors.) After the war both men came back to push-broom jobs in Sequoyah garages.

"We swept our way in," says Dan. "That's always the way for us in this town. They give you the job with the broom. Then you can either keep that broom the rest of your life or you can keep your eyes open and see what else you can do. You find out where things are, if you know what to look for—and are interested. I knew and I was. Pretty soon somebody needs something and you can get it to them. Then they'll need a hand with things on the motors and find out how much you can do. Pretty soon something comes up that has to be done quick—and nobody's there to do it except you. If you're ready, you can start moving away from the broom. But they sure like to keep on paying you sweepers' wages as long as they can."

Dan has ended up as one of the top diesel repairmen in the city, working in the garage of a local big-truck dealer. Joe struck out on his own, working as a handyman around town with an old pickup truck he had bought. Then, for a while, he had his own one-truck moving company but went out of business when he couldn't keep up payments on his truck. After that he did whatever he could in the usual line of clean-up work, occasionally driving produce trucks locally. Finally one of the big long-distance trucking companies that operates out of Sequoyah signed him up several years ago. He now drives heavy-duty, tractor-trailer refrigeration rigs out of Sequoyah to Chicago, Kansas City, Dallas, and Los Angeles.

James Carter has a similar story. Before the war Jim worked as a porter in a fraternity house. Drafted into the Army in 1943, he served in the Pacific theater of operations. After the war he went to work for the Sequoyah Light and Power Company—as a janitor. He kept his eyes open and also took some correspondence courses. Soon he learned enough to begin moonlighting a little, doing wiring and some electrical repair jobs for Spud Davison and other landlords of houses in the Spout Springs neighborhood. Soon people who owned their own homes began to call Jim in to fix things they couldn't handle themselves. This moonlighting business has often been more of an income producer for him than his regular job. However, three years ago the Light and Power Company moved him from his janitor job to a job in their meter-repair shop, where he had been doing a good deal of work, unofficially, for some time.

An interesting breakthrough took place during the 1960s in food-processing plants. Specifically, in 1964 Mrs. Tillie Marks and Mr. Ralph Bush broke the job barrier at the local plant of the National Soup Company. Each seems to have some claim for the honor of being the first Black worker on a food-processing production line. We don't know the details of Bush's entry, but Mrs. Marks told us her story over several cups of hot coffee in her kitchen one summer evening. (She believes that hot coffee is the best way to beat the summer heat.)

"I was working as cook and maid for Mrs. Hetty Scott—her husband owns most of the Scott Car Sales place, and she really bosses the show. She had me come in to help with two parties she gave, evenings, both in one week, just before her daughter got married. Then she wanted to pay me just five dollars extra. I told her it had to be more or I'd quit. So she says, O.K., so quit—and I did. Course, she figured I'd be right back in a couple of days, like what had happened two or three times before. But I went down to Employment Security and put in my name for a fact'ry job. Mr. Coe, he done tried to send me out on some cooking or day-work jobs. But I said, 'No; I'm decided I want to try something different.' So he says,

'O.K., Tillie, you asked for it and I'm going to call your bluff. The Soup Company thinks they want to try to work in some colored on the production line and you can be the first. After about a week I expect those hill people will have you running back here.' So I took the card on that job and went down t' the plant. They asked me a lot of questions and looked at me pretty glum-faced; but they put me out there on the line, finally, cutting up chickens. Those country White women sure looked me over. Didn't say a word to me. So I just said the same right back and went to work. If I needed to know something, I'd ask the foreman at first. I expected the women to treat me mean but they didn't. They didn't really seem to know what to do or say about me. But after a week or so one or two of them started to talk to me and we got along O.K. I did my job and they did theirs. If they talked, I talked. If they didn't, I didn't. So it went along for several months. Then one day, in came a new girl fresh down from Polk County, and made a big to-do about not wanting to drink at the water fountain after a nigger. So, I thought, now the fun will begin. And it did; but not the way I thought. All the White women I'd been working with ganged up on *her*. They just told her to her face to get away from that fountain 'til she learned to be as clean as me. Then maybe they'd let her drink at their fountain. When that happened I knew I'd really made it. Now, I've been working there goin' on four years. Whenever we have a company picnic, pot luck, I fix things and they fix things and we all share what we cook. Now, you may not think this amounts to nothin'. But, you know, those fact'ry people used to say they couldn't hire us because they'd lose all their hill people. Said they's just walk off from their jobs. Well, they didn't and it doesn't seem to be hurting them none."

Ralph Bush apparently got an assembly-line job with the Soup Company (in a different division) at about the same time as Mrs. Marks. Since then, several other Blacks have gone to work for this or other food-processing plants in Sequoyah. Mostly these have been women, since there are more jobs for women in these plants than for men. The jobs involve unskilled or semiskilled types of work, but the breakthrough here expands considerably the range of jobs now available to Black people.

Since 1966 the Community Outreach Agency has played a significant part in changing the job situation. For instance, it has set an example by bringing Negroes onto its staff at semiprofessional, professional, and administrative levels. In addition, the COA is also working indirectly, through the sponsorship of vocational- and business-training programs, to move Black people out of unemployment or unskilled jobs into semiskilled or skilled jobs. All of the recently hired Black office workers have come out of the business-training program. These training programs are available to Whites as well as Blacks, and all classes have, in fact, been integrated.

Sanctions, Customs, and Job Changes

We will conclude our discussion of work by saying a few words about factors, within the local society, that previously set limits on jobs. We will try to answer two questions: Why were these limits effectively maintained before? Why have they been gradually relaxed more recently?

The answer to the first question obviously lies in a fairly strong segregationist, "racist" tradition, which is now much modified. Although Sequoyah and Lincoln County are not "deep South," they have shared the general Southern tradition that Negroes had their proper place in the social and economic scheme. Economically Negroes were thought to be essentially a source of unskilled labor and were simple not hired for other jobs. Employment agencies never sent them to job interviews unless the jobs were thought "appropriate." This was the general rule, to which there were always individual exceptions.

The old tradition persists, but it is no longer universally held. Once it began to lose adherents, new opportunities became available to Black people.

Why is the old tradition about the Negro's proper economic role no longer universally held by Whites in Sequoyah and Lincoln County? Many factors are involved: the changing legal situation concerning the rights of Black people, the influence of mass communication media and their presentation of dramatic ideological changes in the nation, the influence of an increasingly cosmopolitan university. In our opinion the most important factor (though one that reflects the impact of the other factors) is a practical one. Many of the younger generation of native middle- and upper-class White people in Sequoyah recognize that changes now *have* to take place and that the social and economic well-being of Sequoyah, Lincoln County, and western Ozarka depends on a graceful acceptance of change. Otherwise, individuals, businesses, and the region in general will "lose money" and lose expansion opportunities.

Many of these younger White adults attended the high school in 1954 when it was integrated or during the years immediately afterward. They found that integration of a few Black students was quite easy—for the White students. They are thus less fearful of job integration than they might otherwise be. After all, it isn't their jobs that are being integrated. Their changed attitudes are reflected in the opening up of jobs formerly closed to Black people. Actually the changes discussed here are quite modest in scope. The traditional attitude that the Black man's place in the economic sphere is a menial one has by no means completely disappeared.

5

Family and Households

W E HAVE A RECORD of 121 Black households in the Spout Spring's neighborhood. We include individuals living alone as households, for the presence and frequency of one-person households is an important aspect of the Black subculture of Sequoyah. There are 28 such one-person households in the community.

One-Person Households

A majority—sixteen—of the Blacks who live alone are widows or widowers. Seven others are persons separated or divorced from spouses. Five are spinsters or bachelors. Twenty of the Black persons living alone are over fifty years old. Twelve have grown children with families of their own in the community; the younger people have crowded households but maintain close contact with their parents, who are usually pretty independent in their attitudes. It is customary for old people to continue working and to maintain separate residences for as long as they are able. This applies to elderly married couples as well as to widowed or divorced persons. Retirement in Spout Spring is usually based on physical incapacity, not age.

Multi-Person Households

In the Sequoyah Black community there are ninety-three households that have more than one member. The following table summarizes the types of such households and their frequencies:

Nuclear-conjugal families	49 (52.7 percent)
Married couples without children	25 (26.9 percent)
Two-generation matrifocal families	13 (14.0 percent)
Three-generation matrifocal families	3 (3.2 percent)
Patrifocal families	3 (3.2 percent)

Basically the nuclear-conjugal families involve parents and their children. However, some cases also include one or more extra adult relatives in residence besides the basic nuclear family. The thirteen two-generation matrifocal families each includes a woman and her children, without a husband-father present. All three of the three-generation matrifocal families include an older woman with grown daughter(s) and the children of the daughter(s). The three patrifocal families each involve a man with his children or with other closely related younger relatives.

Kinship Ties

The above figures clearly indicate that most Black people of Sequoyah are living in family households. If we discount married couples, as well as persons living alone, there remain sixty-eight households with two or more generations present. We estimate that 389 persons live in such households. In all cases the generations are linked by close kin ties, usually those of parents to children. Moreover, kinship is important far beyond the limits of households. Our data on last names illustrate this. Of seventy-seven last names recorded, we find that twenty-three occur more than once as last names of distinct households. (These figures include the one-person households and the two-person married-couple households.) Ten of the names occur three or more times. The name that occurs most frequently (seven times) is, not unexpectedly, Smith. Three other names occur five times; two occur four times; four occur three times. Kin ties involved with shared last names are mostly quite close, though this is not true of most Smiths.

Matrilateral Extended Families

Of course, kin ties spread beyond the limits of shared last names. They link all but a few members of the community in an overlapping network of relationships. Kin ties among related women (who usually do *not* share last names) are, if anything, even stronger than the relationships among related men. In some cases these *matrilateral* ties are so strong that they form the basis for *extended families*, which link several households with different last names in systems of close cooperation. To some extent these matrilateral extended families resemble the kind of corporate kin groups that anthropologists call *lineages*. However, unlike true lineages, they are difficult to trace genealogically because women's names change after marriage in the usual American pattern. There are some interesting exceptions. These involve cases where women continue to use their maiden names for certain purposes after marriage. This usage involves employment identification and related matters, such as Social Security records and telephone listings. At least one married woman has her telephone listed to a last name that was the name of her maternal grandfather. Thus, for certain economic purposes, she is ignoring the last names of both her husband and her father.

The type of matrilateral kin group described here generally stresses close personal ties among three generations of living women: a mother, her daughters, and her granddaughters. Sisters, nieces, and even grandnieces of the senior woman may sometimes be peripherally involved. Despite the occasional attempt to cling to last names acquired by birth, such families can be identified only in "operational terms"—that is, by the close interaction among the women involved and their family-households.

The "Carter Family"

The kinds of close interaction we speak of are well illustrated by cooperation among several women of the Carter "family." This extended family, which descends from sixty-five-year-old Mary Carter, includes women with four other last names: Mary Carter's three daughters and two grown granddaughters. Although Mary Carter's daughters are all married, they are usually referred to in the Spout Spring neighborhood—and even by White employers—as "the Carter sisters." At present they are the dynamic focus of unity, with their mother the symbol of that unity. There is very close cooperation among the three sisters, which extends to include all other members of their families, as well as those of their grown daughters.

Children of any of the five households involved may be left at any house when their parents are not home; or they may be instructed to go to those houses after school. Most often they are left with—or report to—Mary Carter (their grandmother or great-grandmother, in different cases), who no longer works regularly. She lives with one of her daughters and, in fact, owns the house. Birthday parties or other childrens' parties are put on jointly by all the mothers, with all the children of the five households participating. In addition, guests may include a few nonrelated friends of the children. In spring or summer these parties are usually held in the spacious side yard of Mary Carter's house.

Two of the Carter women, and the husband of one of them, work for a White man who runs a café and caters fraternity and sorority parties. For such parties he needs a good deal of extra help. These parties are usually evening affairs. Therefore, they are good sources of extra income for Black men or women who have regular daytime jobs. The extra help for this White man's catering usually is recruited from the Carter family. All the Carter women, their husbands, and their teen-age children are apt to work at such affairs.

On one occasion one of the grown granddaughters took offense at some sharp words from the White man and walked off the job "in a huff." As soon as her mother and aunts heard of this, they stopped work and began to insist that the whole family walk off the job (although three of them were permanent employees of the White man and valued their jobs highly). They were only prevented from doing so when the White man promised to apologize to the granddaughter. This he later did.

It is necessary to stress here that close interaction among matrilaterally related women does not often involve coresidence. Each of the Carter sisters has lived in Mary's house "in between marriages." But each has since remarried and left the house to set up her own household with her husband and children. After Mary had a mild heart attack, her eldest daughter, whose second husband had died recently, moved back into Mary's house, mainly "to watch out for" her.

Matrifocal Families

Although matrilateral extended families in the Sequoyah Black community are not residential units as such, a few do have a matrifocal core household. The Carter family situation just described illustrates this well. The matrilateral unit involves five distinct households. Four of these are nuclear-conjugal families. But the fifth, the one now residing in Mary's house, can be technically defined as a three-generation matrifocal family, including as it does Mary Carter, her eldest daughter, and this daughter's two youngest children.

Altogether there are sixteen matrifocal families in the Sequoyah Black community. They can be divided between two subtypes—two-generation matrifocal families and three-generation matrifocal families. Typically these have different developmental histories.

The two-generation subtype of matrifocal family usually consists of a young mother with children but without a husband-father. In the Sequoyah Black community, these households are the result of the breakup of early first marriages. This leaves young women as heads of families with very small children. In most cases such families soon return to the nuclear-conjugal category with the second marriage of the mother. Second marriages are apparently more stable in this community than first marriages, especially if the husband is old enough to be economically and emotionally well established.

At any given time, there will be from twelve to twenty two-generation matrifocal families in the Sequoyah Black community.

The three-generation subtype of matrifocal family develops when the core household of a matrilateral extended family takes back into it a daughter and her children. Sometimes this occurs when a young wife has lost a husband through divorce or dispute. These cases are essentially temporary, just as the two-generation matrifocal families tend to be. But when an older woman returns to the core household with her younger children, it is likely to be a more permanent situation. The reasons for returning may vary. In the case of the Carters, it was the death of a husband and the illness of Mary Carter that combined to bring about the return.

The Baker Family

In the Baker family a somewhat different series of events brought about the development of a three-generation matrifocal family. At present there are ten persons residing in the Baker house: four adult women and six children ranging in age from six to fourteen years old. The founder of this household is Willy Mae

Baker, aged about seventy, who owns the house. She is a sweet-tempered, agree-able matriarch, who has always wanted to have as many of her descendants as possible living close to her. Underneath the amiable aspect of her personality is a very strong will. She owns the house, a rather large, about sixty-year-old, wooden frame building, which has been remodeled or added to several times and is in very good repair. It was originally purchased by Willy Mae's husband, Ray Baker, who has been dead for about ten years. He had been a railroad porter until he retired in 1950, and during much of his active life had, of necessity, been away from home a great deal. Though he had always provided well, it had been up to Willy Mae to take the responsibility of household and family affairs in Sequoyah. She thus acquired a strong sense of independence but also a strong psychological dependence on the presence of a large family in the house.

Willy Mae was Ray Baker's second wife. Ray met Willy Mae at the upper end of his railroad run, in Kansas City, where she worked in a restaurant run by her brother. This was around 1920. Ray and Willy Mae were married in Kansas City but after their first daughter was born Ray brought the family back to Sequoyah and bought the house Willy Mae owns today.

It should be stressed that the Baker marriage was a stable one and that this household began as a strong nuclear-conjugal family. Willy Mae was always somewhat jealous of Ray's first wife because Ray frequently visited his two chil-dren, both boys, by this first wife. These visits were rather easy to fit into his schedule, as Ray continued for many years to work on trains that made a crew change in Texarkana. However, he was devoted to Willy Mae, to their chil-dren, and eventually to their grandchildren. In addition to being a good provider he invested his money wisely in improvements on the house in Sequoyah. After his death his wife and daughters continued this policy of "keeping the place up," so that it is one of the most attractively furnished houses in the Spout Spring neighborhood.

Ray and Willy Mae had four children, all girls. The eldest moved to Chicago after she grew up. There she got a job as a maid and, later, housekeeper for a wealthy White family. She is married to a fellow employee. They occasionally visit Spout Spring during vacations. Members of the Baker family sometimes visit them in Chicago. The other three daughters remained in Sequoyah. The second daughter, Dorothy, married James Carter and with him has established a stable nuclear-conjugal family with seven children. The other two daughters, Ruth and Della, have each been married twice and divorced twice. Each is a dynamic and sexually attractive woman. But both now live with their mother—and their younger children—in the Baker house. This household became a three-generation matrifocal family during the late 1950s, even while Ray Baker was still living (he died in 1959). But the makeup of the household has varied somewhat. Both Ruth and Della have, at different times, lived elsewhere during periods of mar-riage. However, both have been in the household continuously since 1963. The situation seems now to have a permanent character.

Ruth and Della Baker are both very competent cooks and housekeepers, highly respected by the White families for whom they work. Both are very independent-minded, and their divorces resulted from clashes with the equally strong personalities of their husbands. Ruth has three children still living with her; Della has two. Moreover, one of Della's resident children is a teen-age daughter who is married and has a baby daughter. Since her husband is in the Army at present, she lives "at home" with her mother, aunt, and grandmother, as well as her brother and cousins.

Patrifocal Families

A patrifocal type of family household occurs when a man's wife dies, or leaves him without taking the children, and he maintains a household for his children without remarrying. We have a record of three patrifocal households in the Sequoyah Black community. Two are headed by widowers; the third is headed by a divorced man.

Most men of the Sequoyah Black community are very devoted to their children and will try to keep them together after the death of a mother if they can. This characteristic is basic to the existence of patrifocal families. Relatively few such families occur, however, because men tend to remarry sooner or later after the death of a wife—and also because young children usually stay with the mother after a divorce.

fathers' feeling about children

The Smith Family

The most stable and enduring of the patrifocal families we know about is actually from the past. It was maintained for over twenty years by James Smith, a baker. Mr. Smith was born on a farm in the southern end of Lincoln County just before the turn of the century. His father, Abe Smith, moved the family into Sequoyah around 1905 when James was quite a small boy. James thus grew up in the Spout Spring neighborhood at a time when it was very small and semirural in character. The Smith family had a truck garden every year and also raised hogs. Abe Smith collected garbage from White families in town in order to feed the hogs. The family lived partly on what it raised and partly on the cash earned by the sale of vegetables and hog meat. The house Abe Smith started to build grew slowly and remained incomplete for over ten years.

In 1916, before the United Stated entered World War I, James Smith enlisted in the Army. During the war he was sent to cooks' and bakers' schools and then served as a cook at one of the big training bases. After the war and the completion of his enlistment, James Smith went to work as a railroad diner chef. He held this job for many years and made enough to be able to send money home to his father, to help have the family house completed. Abe Smith died in 1926, and his son returned to Sequoyah to live, taking over the house his father had built and taking care of his mother and sisters, who continued to live there for a number of years. James married soon after returning to Sequoyah and brought his wife to this house from her home in Rush Hill. In 1927 he quit work with the railroad altogether and took a job as chef at a large resort hotel near Sequoyah. This work was seasonal—from late spring to early fall. During the winters he either loafed or took jobs cooking in local restaurants.

When the resort business went bad during the Depression, the hotel closed down. However, James Smith was lucky enough to get back his railroad job, which he kept until World War II. Then he got a job in a large commercial bakery that had just opened up in Sequoyah. He continued to work there until he retired in 1962. The manager of the bakery, a man of rather strong anti-Negro sentiments, admitted to us that Smith was "a real professional" and well worth the top wages he earned.

James Smith's wife died during the war, leaving him with a twelve-year-old daughter, two sons, eight and five years old, and another daughter, an infant of two years. It was at this time that he left his railroad job for the second time, to be closer to his children. He had a little help from his wife's sister, who also lived in Sequoyah. But she had a large family of her own to care for, so she was not able to do much more than lend James moral support, sympathy, and advice. On the other hand, he found that he could depend a lot on his oldest girl to take care of the younger children while he worked. He taught her to cook meals when he could not be at home. The children were left alone a lot of the time, but "the neighbors looked in on them and Josie knew to go next door and ask for help if she needed it."

By the time Smith retired from the bakery, all his children were grown and married. His oldest girl had married a local boy when she was eighteen, and the couple had lived for a while in her father's house. Her husband, a professional Army man, tried civilian life for a while after World War II and during this time married Josie. But he was called back into the Army during the Korean War and has stayed in ever since. He is now a master sergeant and will soon retire.

Josie lived with her husband on or near Army posts for a while after he got back from Korea, but later they built one of the better and newer houses in the Spout Spring neighborhood, about two blocks from her father's place. Josie and her three children live there most of the time, and her husband comes home there whenever he has leave. Even while she lived near Army posts, Josie took her three children home to her father's house for frequent visits—usually short ones except for a visit of several weeks in the summer. Josie's oldest, a girl, is now fully grown and attending college; the other two children, a boy and a girl, are teen-agers who still look in on their grandfather to see how he is doing.

James Smith's two sons completed high school in another city and went into the Army in the early 1950s. Both served one enlistment, then settled down with their wives, whom they'd met while in the service in the cities their wives came from. One son moved back to Sequoyah for a while but for the past five years has been living in Memphis, Tennessee, where he runs a barber shop. The other son has lived and worked for years in Los Angeles, where he is now a policeman; he returns home to Sequoyah only to visit his father, sister, and other relatives there. The youngest child, a daughter, remained at home to keep house for her father until she married at twenty-two, a relatively late age for a Spout Spring girl. Her husband, like her father, is a baker. She and her husband live just a few doors away and, like Josie and her children, look in on Mr. Smith every day.

Because James Smith had good training and skill in a calling that was much in demand and has always been considered "appropriate" for Negroes, he was never seriously frustrated by the job barrier. He was able to work continuously, even during the Depression when a great many White men were desperate for work.

 ## Marital Relations

Our long account of the Knight family (Chapter 3) and the shorter accounts of the Carter, Baker, and Smith families all serve to illustrate more than just the variations in household patterns. They give insights into recurring aspects of adult personal adjustment in the Sequoyah Black community and hint at tensions in male-female relationships.

Most Black Sequoyah women work and contribute significantly to family incomes. Their contributions in a good many cases equal, and in a few cases exceed, their husbands'. Generally speaking, women do not have any strong reason to feel absolute economic dependence on their husbands. If anything, their incomes are spent more for basic necessities, while their husbands tend to spend more on supplementary luxuries. Women also have strongly institutionalized roles in matrilateral extended families as well as in groups based on non-kin principles (see Chapter 6). This is especially true in the churches (though the highest-status positions, preachers and deacons, are mainly held by men). All these factors operate to make the wife's role in the family and the woman's role in the community very secure. Considerable competence in cooking, housekeeping, and child-rearing is characteristic.

However, men are not typically subordinate and "browbeaten." They too contribute significantly to family incomes. Their contributions equal or exceed their wives' in a majority of cases. However, young men are generally at a disadvantage here; their incomes are often less than their wives' (though this is changing as the job situation in Sequoyah changes). Men's roles in family households are about as strongly institutionalized as women's. This is probably a holdover from the rural past, when the agricultural households were male-dominated work teams. Although men have recently had fewer strong roles in local non-kin groups, most of them have served in the armed services and have derived a sense of masculine adequacy from such service. Moreover, the recent trend to jobs related to the servicing of motor cars also supports strongly masculine identity.

Thus, husband-wife relationships depend a great deal on individual personality characteristics and special circumstances. Nevertheless, some generalizations can be made. Young wives are apt to give voice to the fact that they bring in more income than their husbands, who tend to react violently against being reminded of this. This seems to be the main reason that so many first marriages break up. Some women continue to be feisty and aggressive throughout their lives; but the majority mellow and develop egalitarian or even apparently submissive wifely roles. Older men also seem to have developed greater patience, along with the security of better incomes, though a few continue in the aggressiveness of their youth. There are even a few men who have developed docile, subordinate roles in their marriages. On the whole, however, both men and women are proud and have strong self-images. In most marriages, husband and wife achieve a kind of balance of role expectations, involving tacit mutual agreements about areas in which each will be dominant. These expectations vary from marriage to marriage, are never perfectly in balance, and rarely conform exactly to conventional models.

Parent-Child Relations

Sequoyah Black men give a great deal of time to their children and tend to be more permissive toward them than the women are. Mothers are apt to be strong disciplinarians, particularly toward daughters, from whom they expect more responsibility than from sons. The men do not seem to make this distinction and are less likely than their wives to exact responsibility from preschool children.

Once children are in school they see less of their parents but much more of older relatives, especially grandmothers, who care for them when the parents work. Parents try to compensate for lost time with their children by making much of weekends and holidays as family occasions.

Sibling Relations

Sibling rivalry is very stong and very openly expressed among young children. It seems to be especially channeled along sex lines, that is, between brothers and sisters. Brothers are somewhat more likely to get along with each other; the same is true of sisters. This is especially true as children grow older.

After children grow up and reach full adult status, the overt expression of sibling rivalry tends to be suppressed and to be replaced often by close friendship and mutual support. This is especially true among sisters and is one of the strong supporting factors underlying the matrilateral extended families discussed earlier, as well as the occasional three-generation matrifocal families. Adult women are very supportive of younger brothers, male cousins, and nephews who may have left their parents' homes and are struggling to establish themselves. Often they provide these young men with a place to stay for days or even weeks on end. Older brothers or brothers of like age get along much better with their sisters than they did as youngsters. To some degree they can count on mutual help and assistance in life crises; but there is less need for such cooperation among older persons who have established themselves in stable family situations. After they are adults, brothers do not work as closely with each other as their sisters do.

However, they do get along well with each other in visiting and in friendly drinking at Grant's Place.

Sometimes sibling rivalry flares up again in later years. This may result from disputes about property, but sometimes it reflects clashes between the men's wives and sisters. Such clashes are socially disapproved by the community; it is thought that close relatives ought to suppress such rivalries and resolve differences in a "decent way." Despite this ideal norm these clashes do occur fairly often.

Socialization

Black children who have lived only in Sequoyah are somewhat less aggressive and "mean" than Black children who have lived for some time elsewhere. However, all Black children in the community are very expressive. For instance, these children communicate verbally very effectively in the preschool years, both within the family· and to outsiders. Babies are constantly held and talked to by parents, siblings, and other relatives. Their vocal responses are encouraged and "bragged on." Toddlers and preschool children in general have much interaction with each other and with the older children who care for them, as well as with parents and other adults. We find Black children more effectively socialized than children of low-income White families. In fact, they seem rather like children in middle-class Sequoyah White families, at least during preschool or early school years. That their mothers often have a good deal to do with the care and feeding of middle-class White children of preschool and early school years may be related to this.

Most children now go to high school, though all do not graduate. Most boys are very athletically inclined, and several have been outstanding athletes at Sequoyah High School since its integration over fifteen years ago. A record of athletic achievement has made the high school experience somewhat more satisfactory for boys than for girls, who feel that they are socially ostracized. However, teen-agers and young adults of both sexes seem to be in a state of rebellion against their parents and the White-dominated society. Related to this may be the fact that there are now no Blacks on any of the high school teams. Possibly this is because there are presently no competent athletes among the few Black boys between the ages of fourteen and nineteen. At any time Blacks in this age range tend to be few in number simply because the total Black population of the city is so small; but some Black leaders tell us that a recently appointed coach has imposed an unofficial boycott and that Black boys simply do not make the teams. (In the summer of 1970, we were informed that no Black athletes have made any SHS teams since our research.)

Youth rebellion does not appear to be very goal-oriented yet; that is, it consists of great emphasis on verbal symbols, clothing styles, and Afro hairstyles. There has been an increase in juvenile delinquency, though the rate does not seem to be any greater than among young Whites. Certain individuals among the teen-agers and young adults have made effective career beginnings; hence the comments concerning lack of goal orientation must be strongly qualified. However,

Boys cutting through back yards on way home from school.

most young people who have made such effective career beginnings have had to leave Sequoyah to find their opportunities.

Marriage and Sex

In our interviews concerning families and households, we made no attempt to distinguish consensual unions from more formal marriages. We felt that questions concerning this distinction could have jeopardized our chances of getting other, less sensitive, types of information. Therefore, we have taken all domestic arrangements at face value. If a man and a woman are living together and she uses his last name, we assume this to be a marriage. Even in those cases where the woman uses her maiden name for certain purposes, as previously discussed, we still regard the relationship as a marriage if she uses the man's last name for other purposes. In such cases, for instance, the children always seem to take the man's last name. Thus, we have not developed any systematic data on relative frequency of consensual versus formal marriages. We do have the general impression that in most (perhaps all) of the well-established households we have observed, the marriages are formal ones. On the other hand, our data suggest that early marriages are sometimes actually trial marriages on a consensual basis and that such marriages are placed on a more formal basis if children are born. Our data do not indicate how frequently early marriages are trial consensual unions.

With respect to more casual sexual liaisons, whether premarital or extramarital, we have also made no special efforts to gather information. However, special efforts are not needed to get an impression of such matters. We can report that this is not a prudish or puritanical community. Men and women of the Sequoyah Black community are not unduly inhibited sexually. On the other hand, they are not so uninhibited as to be blatantly promiscuous. These are general statements; there are individual exceptions in both directions.

Vague reports circulating among "sporting elements" in the White population of Sequoyah suggest that there may be some Black prostitutes. The only basis for these rumors seems to involve two or three young women who are divorced or separated and who may supplement their incomes in this way. Other Black women report, with amused contempt, that they are propositioned quite often by White men. This does not, of course, preclude the possibility that they —or other Black women—might sometimes react more favorably to less mercenary approaches. But the affairs we have actually heard about, whether in rumor or in confidential report, involved only Black people and had no commercial connotations.

We have heard of only one possible instance of homosexuality. This report involved a young man who apparently is not a native of Sequoyah.

Kin Terms and Exogamy

The kinship system and terminology differ in no discernible way from the general patterns in the United States. There is no evidence that "uncle" and "aunt" terms are currently extended to non-kin, by either Whites or Blacks, in referring to respected Black elders. However, until the 1920s or 1930s such terms were applied to respected Blacks by Sequoyah Whites.

Rules of exogamy are more implicit than explicit. They apply bilaterally with about equal force. Marriages do not take place between members of the named patrilateral or unnamed matrilateral extended families described earlier.

Young girls heading home from school playground take short cut through unpaved alley leading into The Valley.

It is thought unwise for persons with the same last name to marry, since last names usually imply relatively close patrilateral kinship. Further, our data suggest a taboo against overfrequent marriages between the same two families; for example, after the marriage of Bill Knight and Sheila Carter, it would be thought advisable that no other Knight marry a Carter for a generation or two. Our information on this is fragmentary and possibly misleading. We do know of at least one case where two marriages of this sort took place within only a scant generation span and we heard a comment questioning the propriety of the second of these marriages.

Despite the general implicit rules concerning exogamy, a majority of Spout Spring marriages take place between members of the community. This is possible because marriages to distant relatives (beyond first cousin) are not disapproved unless they involve the name taboos mentioned earlier. Since there are over seventy different last names recorded in the community, it is quite obvious that a good deal of choice remains for selection of marriage partners.

6

Non-Kin Groups

As our discussion in Chapter 5 indicates, family households and extended kin groups are of great importance within the Sequoyah Black community. Within the households, individuals establish most of their personal identities. In addition, these family and kin groups form a network of interrelations that permeate and, in a sense, *establish* the community. However, there are other groups, not based on kinship, that are also important within this community.

Types of Groups

Sociologists and anthropologists often draw a distinction between formal and informal social groups. Formal groups usually have names, designated offices, scheduled meetings, specific criteria for membership, and one or more definite purposes (often implied or stated in the group's name). By way of contrast, informal groups usually lack names, offices, scheduled meetings, overt membership criteria, and overtly stated purposes. However, careful analysis of informal groups often reveals different personal roles, some regular rhythm of interaction, identifiable participants in interaction, and identifiable purposes. This chapter will be devoted to a discussion of formal and informal groups in the Black population of Sequoyah. Our information about formal groups is naturally more complete than about informal groups. We have drawn some generalizations from it.

Most of the older formal groups in the Sequoyah Black community are church-oriented or otherwise based on rigid membership-limiting criteria. These groups also tend to be accommodationist in character; that is, they implicitly or explicitly recognize racial segregation in a White-dominated society, and they represent institutionalized methods of accommodation to such a society. Accommodation involves both organization and goals. Organization is on a segregated basis: all group members are Black. Goals are, or at least traditionally have been, limited to ends that were possible and permitted in a White-dominated society.

51

Methodist Church.

Another important characteristic of older formal groups is that they do not represent communitywide interaction patterns. This follows from their limited memberships. However, there is a partial exception to this generalization: the Civic Club, which has had a long history and has had obvious communitywide aspirations from time to time.

In contrast to the older "accommodationist" formal organizations, several secular organizations have emerged in Sequoyah during the past ten years. These attempt to identify common interests of the Black community and to recruit membership widely from that community. In addition, they tend to be biracial in membership and to have strongly assimilationist characteristics. That is, organization and purposes are, among other things, aimed at the integration of Black people into United States society in terms of social and economic equality. They seek especially to achieve this integration locally.

Informal groups, almost by their very nature, tend to be restricted with respect to both participation and scope of interest. This is especially true among

Baptist Church.

cliques of older people. However, some of the newer cliques may have potential for development into a third type of formal group, one that is communitywide in scope but separatist in character—that is, militant and racially exclusive. Some of the new cliques involve teen-agers; others involve young adults; still others may involve both. Both the exclusively adult cliques and the exclusively teen-age cliques tend to be largely hedonistic; but some teen-age cliques have recently begun to grope toward goals that link them to the emergent nationwide values of the Black movement. These groups have potential for coalescing into formal separatist groups. To do this, however, they would have to link up successfully with young-adult cliques. Only thus could they develop an effective permanent organization and consistent goals. So far this has not happened.

Churches and Church Groups

Each of the three Black churches in Sequoyah involves a complex of closely knit formal groups, as well as some informal groups. Each church congregation is, of itself, a group. It has a minister, a board of deacons, and various committees. Each congregation can be divided into numerous smaller formal groups of three main types: (1) boards of deacons, made up mostly of men; (2) Sunday school and Bible school groups, which include both sexes; and (3) women's groups. There are also some informal or formal singing groups: choirs, choruses, and some very innovative small singing groups made up of teen-agers or young adults. Both sexes are represented in such singing groups, although any one group is usually made up either of males or of females. The style of these singing groups seems similar to that of currently popular professional groups and is probably influenced by them. On a national basis, professional groups probably borrow from the religious musical groups.

The Methodist and Baptist churches are both old churches. We have been unable to establish clearly dates of origin, but they both go back to the nineteenth century. There is indirect evidence that both churches may derive from pre-Civil War "slave congregations."

Church of Christ. The men of the congregation have worked cooperatively to convert this former dwelling into a church building.

Traditionally, the Methodist church has been the leading church in the Sequoyah Black community in terms of both membership and prestige. In 1928 it had seventy-five members to the Baptists' thirty. At present its claimed membership is over a hundred.

On the other hand, the Baptist church, with a claimed membership of only ninety-three, has a larger attendance and is more dynamic than the Methodist church. This may be related to the fact that the Baptist church does not have a resident minister but is served by temporary lay preachers, although most members seem to think they prefer a resident clergyman.

The Methodist church is going through a rather static phase. The minister, Reverend L. J. Allen, is an elderly man who served many years in southern Arkansas churches. Three years ago he was called from retirement to take over the Methodist pastorate in Sequoyah. Allen lives in Sequoyah, in the parsonage next door to the church, on Birch Avenue.

The Church of Chirst was founded about six years ago. Originally a few Black families attended the big Church of Christ near the Square, a predominantly White institution. As more Black families joined the faith, a separate Negro church was established, with the aid of funds from the White church. A retired railroad man, Brother Graham Shaw, assumed leadership of the congregation soon after its founding. Brother Shaw has been markedly successful both as organizer and as preacher. At present membership in the congregation numbers around sixty, and attendance is high every Sunday. Services are held in a former residence in the mixed neighborhood south of the Valley. The men of the congregation have remodeled the building inside and out, and it has gradually taken on a very churchlike aspect. The Church of Christ is at once the most dynamic Black congregation in Sequoyah and the most conservative in theology and social values. Although new in time, it conforms to the older, more traditional pattern of formal group structure.

Other Older Groups

Outside the context of church activities, there are some significant friendship groups among women. In a few cases these are formal groups, with names and fairly regular monthly meetings held in the homes of the members. Membership in such named groups is quite specific and limited. The Deborah Club, for instance, has only ten members. If one woman resigns or dies, another woman is chosen to replace her. The main purpose seems to be the preservation of regular social interaction among the members, most of whom have been friends since childhood. This appears to be the purpose of all such secular formal women's groups. There are numerous less formal friendship groups, loose cliques of women based on visiting patterns among neighbors. Quite often they involve related women and are neighborhood expressions of the matrilateral extended families discussed in the preceding chapter.

There have been a number of attempts to set up formal associations confined to male membership. None are currently active. Old newspaper files yield information about a Negro Businessmen's Club that existed back in the 1920s. This club evolved into the present Civic Club. Two other formal men's associations, of more recent vintage, were a Negro fraternal lodge and a Negro veterans' organization. The fraternal organization once had a building on Second Street and held regular meetings there. The building burned down in the 1950s, but the lot it once occupied is still owned by the lodge. Apparently because of the loss of the building, the lodge is now nearly inactive; however, a few men are still identified as members, and small meetings are occasionally held.

The veterans' organization was founded immediately after World War II. For a time it attracted a considerable number of young Black veterans, but it died out in the early 1950s. While it was active, the organization sponsored evening classes for veterans in the Carver School. These aimed at giving returning veterans a chance to use their GI Bill education rights to complete high school or to take technical training of a vocational type. Relatively few of the men stuck with the classes long enough to complete them or to derive much benefit from them. As interest in the classes faded out, the veterans' organization itself seemed to deteriorate. It no longer exists on even an inactive basis.

The one older organization that has attempted to represent all the people in the Sequoyah Black community has been the Civic Club. As we have already mentioned, the roots of the Civic Club go back to the nearly forgotten Negro Businessmen's Club of the 1920s. We do not know just when it broadened its membership basis; but it is clear that for the past thirty years the Club has had both male and female members. Theoretically all adult Negroes in Sequoyah are eligible for membership. In practice, only a small number of persons regularly attends meetings or otherwise identifies with the Club.

The Civic Club's purposes include promoting the general welfare of the Black population of Sequoyah, which is conceived to be a community. However, this interest has not developed a clear and significant focus. At present the club is most effective in organizing and promoting certain "housekeeping" activities, such as efforts to improve property, keep unsightly trash off streets, and maintain the Negro cemetery. Members have a strong concern for the image of the Spout Spring neighborhood.

For many years the Civic Club owned and maintained a building on the grounds of the old Carver School. Club meetings were held there, and the building was also made available for other activities of community interest. This building has recently been torn down and the school grounds have been sold to the Sequoyah Housing Authority, which will soon build a low-cost housing project there. A new community center is being proposed as part of this housing project. However, the housing project is to be integrated, and the community center may be reserved for the sole use of project residents. Therefore, the loss of its building is a threat to the continued existence of the Civic Club.

Newer Groups

Here we will discuss groups of generally more recent origin, whose interests and purposes are broader and more assimilationist in character than those of the older groups. However, it is suitable to begin this discussion by considering some possible new directions the Civic Club may take, if it survives. Although the active membership is still quite small and only intermittently very active, some current issues have revived interest and create the possibility of a revitalized Civic Club. If the members choose, they may well use these issues to transform the club into a much more significant organization.

New Issues and the Civic Club

One of the issues giving the Civic Club potential new importance is the need to have a minority group representative on the Board of Directors of the county Community Outreach Agency (COA). The constitution of that organization, as revised in 1968, provides for a minority group representative and assigns to the Civic Club responsibility for selecting him. In July of 1968 the Civic Club first performed this function by sponsoring a meeting at which Mrs. Annie Mae Sibley was elected to the COA Board. This meeting was not considered to be a meeting of the club, since the club did not choose to use this as an occasion for expanding active membership. Nevertheless, the club will continue to have the responsibility for sponsoring an election for this purpose every two years, as long as both it and the COA exist.

Another issue that may increase the effectiveness of the Civic Club is a current drive to get certain streets paved in the Spout Spring neighborhood. Again the COA is involved; the initiative for this drive came, most recently at least, from Joe Carter, a Black man who is Director of the COA's East Sequoyah Neighborhood Center. In an attempt to stimulate mass support for the paving project, Mr. Carter asked the Civic Club to sponsor a meeting at which the project could be discussed and strategy planned. The club did sponsor the meeting, which took place in its building, but did not treat this as a meeting of its membership. However, the Paving Committee that was formed at the meeting was considered by some to be a committee of the club. Others considered it to be an autonomous committee representing only the people living on the streets involved. The Paving Committee later reported back to a second meeting sponsored by the club, giving the results of its conference with the Sequoyah City Manager and the Street Superintendent. The second mass meeting continued the existence of the committee and assigned further functions to it. The sheer need for a permanent organizational base from which such committees can operate may force the club to assume gradually that role in this and similar situations. For this role, however, another formal group is also a candidate: the East Sequoyah Neighborhood Council, which is a biracial offshoot of the COA.

The Sequoyah Good Neighbor Council

During the first half of the 1960s, the most influential formal group involving Black membership was the Sequoyah Good Neighbor Council (SGNC). The

SGNC is a biracial association, but its principal concern is the civil rights of Sequoyah Negroes. Further, it has placed emphasis on the Black population of Sequoyah as a *community*; it has enrolled as members a rather large number of Negroes, who have been at least as active as the White members.

The general membership of the SGNC plays a rather passive role most of the year. However, there is a consistently active core group of about five Black members and five White members. The Black activists are generally persons who are also active members of the Civic Club. The White activists are usually OSU professors or their wives. The Council, which has been in existence since around 1950, reached its peak influence between 1960 and 1965.

The activities of the SGNC generally involve civil rights in some way. For instance, the Council investigates specific cases of alleged discrimination against Black individuals or groups. It attempts to deal with such cases in a moderate and persuasive way, using a technique of "quiet desegregation," which has also been tacitly accepted by Sequoyah civic leaders and the city's only newspaper. The SGNC also organizes panel-discussion workshops and other programs once or twice a year for the benefit of the whole SGNC membership and other interested citizens. Such workshops or programs are usually well attended by both Blacks and Whites.

An even more useful function of the SGNC may have been that of leadership training. It has provided opportunities for Blacks to occupy actively leadership roles in a biracial context. Several Black leaders who have read early drafts of this chapter have pointed out to us that both the Methodist and Baptist churches have had formal programs of leadership training and that they consider themselves to be products of these training programs. They point out that most of the SGNC Black activists were persons who had already been trained in church leadership. However, it seems to us that SGNC has at least provided a "graduate course," in a broader context than that provided by the churches.

Another important accomplishment of the SGNC has been the successful establishment in Lincoln County of a community-action agency recognized and substantially funded by the U.S. Office of Economic Opportunity. The SGNC cannot be given sole credit for this achievement, but it played a significant part in making it possible. This was done mainly through the sponsorship of a workshop on poverty in Sequoyah in the fall of 1965. The moving spirit in setting up and directing this workshop was a young White professor at OSU, Abe Morton. The workshop generated so much interest that a communitywide committee was established to work on the project of getting a community-action program set up in the County and funded. Professor Morton was chairman of this committee, which included other White members of the OSU faculty, Blacks, and a number of young men of the permanent Sequoyah White population who brought considerable support to the project. In a sense, these young Sequoyah men represented a kind of "Young Turk" rebellion within the power structure or Establishment of Sequoyah. At this same time the group was also active in pushing for a change in the form of municipal government in the city. Within a year both its objectives—an anti-poverty agency and the establishment of the city-manager form of municipal government—were attained. These were achieved by an unofficial coalition of various interest groups, including the SGNC, the League of Women Voters, the Junior Chamber of Commerce, labor leaders, and community-oriented members of the Black community.

The Community Outreach Agency

The Lincoln County Community Outreach Agency (COA) was established in 1966, as a nonprofit organization incorporated under the laws of the state of Ozarka. It receives the majority of its financial backing from federal funds, channeled through the U.S. Office of Economic Opportunity and the Department of Labor. Subsequent to its organization, the COA and groups directly or indirectly sponsored by it have been as important to the Sequoyah Black community as the SGNC and the Civic Club. This has been the case partly because the COA has significantly influenced the economic status of some Blacks and aspires to do so for all Blacks in Sequoyah. Perhaps just as important, it has provided participation opportunities for Blacks through its various affiliated groups. Significantly most Blacks who have participated effectively in such groups have previously had similar experience as members of either the Civic Club or SGNC—or both.

The original Board of Directors of the COA had a Black member, Mr. Ben Albert, one of three persons elected to represent the city of Sequoyah. Three other Negroes have since served on the Board: Mr. Ralph Cash, Mrs. Lenore Carter, and Mrs. Annie Mae Sibley. There has been Black representation on subordinate or affiliated boards and committees in connection with COA activities. One such group, an entirely Negro group, was the Birch Avenue Neighborhood Council, which was formed in the spring of 1966 and lasted until the summer of 1968.

The Neighborhood Council

The Birch Avenue Council was one of seven such councils organized in Lincoln County during the spring and summer of 1966. These were intended to be grass-roots associations of poor people. According to the official ideology of the federal Office of Economic Opportunity, the function of such groups was to express the felt needs of the poor and thus give direction to the whole anti-poverty program. However effective this approach may be elsewhere, it has not worked well in Lincoln County, for reasons that we feel are characteristic of the regional subculture.

The only one of the original seven councils to produce, on its own initiative, a clearly formulated set of proposals for the anti-poverty program was the all-Negro Birch Avenue Council. This set of proposals was developed by a committee of the council during the summer and was then considered by the whole council and passed as recommendations. They were subsequently submitted to the Board of Directors of the COA. Most of these proposals were eventually adopted or in some manner incorporated into COA policy and organizational structure. Among the more important results of these proposals were: the appointment of low-income persons as trainees for COA staff positions; the establishment of the staff positions of Neighborhood Aide and Community Organizer; the setting up of Neighborhood or Area Centers in Sequoyah and elsewhere in the county; and the establishment of the Sequoyah Child Care Center for preschool children of low-income families.

In contrast to this quite effective early action of the Birch Avenue Neighborhood Council, the other six original COA Councils in the county tended to be relatively ineffective or, at best, mere sounding boards for proposals initiated elsewhere, often by the COA staff. In our opinion there were two reasons for this lack of participation: (1) very few poor people joined the councils or attended meetings; and (2) those who did attend council meetings did not want to get themselves involved by making suggestions. Underlying these inhibitions, we feel, are certain cultural characteristics of the western Ozarka population—a dislike for formal organization and a strong feeling of personal autonomy, which caused most people to reject the label "poor," even though they had low incomes. (See our discussion of "themes" in Chapter 8.)

The Birch Avenue Council was never a large-scale organization in terms of attendance and active participation by poor people. Its members—those who attended meetings—fluctuated between five and fifty persons. The core group of active members usually numbered between ten and fifteen. Most of these were persons who were also active in the Civic Club, the SGNC, or in church-related groups. However, this council did have a kind of indirect grass-roots character; its active members came to be regarded as collective spokesmen for the Black community. Such tacit recognition of the Council's role did not come easily or quickly and was never universal. During the winter and spring of 1968, the Black community, and the Council, were seriously split by a bitter policy controversy within the COA. This controversy involved the firing of several dissident staff members, led by a White woman with many strong supporters in the Black community. This dissident group bitterly denounced the Executive Director and Board of Directors of the agency on grounds that essentially involved differences of opinion concerning administrative action. In the lack of initiative from local councils, the Executive Director, backed by the Board, was taking the responsibility for setting up programs of vocational education. The dissident group felt that efforts should first be devoted to community organization and that after such organization had taken place, the true wishes of the poor would become known. Incidental charges of various kinds were made on both sides, with criticisms concerning competence and integrity. These charges created great bitterness. Thus, when the two Black members then serving on the COA Board of Directors voted in support of the position taken by the Executive Director and the majority of other Board members, they were subjected to considerable criticism within the Black community. One of these members was the Birch Avenue Council's representative on the Board; the other was one of the three Board members representing the City of Sequoyah at large.

The East Sequoyah Area Council

From the point of view of the COA, there was one great defect in the Birch Avenue Council; it was a *de facto* segregated body. That is, most White residents of the Birch Avenue target area simply ignored the existence of the Council or refused to join because they thought of it as a Negro-dominated organization. Therefore, when the organizational structure of the COA was revamped in 1968 (partly as a result of the controversy described earlier), the Birch Avenue Council was replaced by a new council, based on the entire east side of the Sequoyah School District. This new council came to be called the East Sequoyah Area Council (but it is usually referred to as a neighborhood council). The new council has a seven-man Policy Advisory Board with both Black and White members. A majority of those who have participated in council meetings have been Blacks. But, interestingly, they have elected a White woman to their two most important offices. This woman is Mrs. Susan Martin, a local civic leader and churchwoman who has close and sympathetic ties to the people of the Black community. She was first elected as the new council's representative to the COA Board of Directors in July of 1968. Later, she was also elected to be Chairman of the council's Policy Advisory Board. The intent of the council, in these actions, seems to have been to emphasize the biracial aspirations of the new organizational setup. Other offices of the council are held by Blacks.

Black COA Staff Members

At present the permanent professional and semiprofessional staff of the COA includes three Black members: Mrs. Daphne Newton, Community Organizer in Sequoyah; Mr. Jack Carter, East Sequoyah Neighborhood Center Director; and Mrs. Lucymae Norman, Assistant Director of the Sequoyah Child Care Center (SCCC). Various other Blacks have served as volunteers or as temporary employees. The SCCC has at least four permanent nonprofessional Black employees.

Blacks have, as a matter of fact, been overrepresented in COA activities, compared to poor Whites. The majority of low-income people in Sequoyah and in Lincoln County are Whites. But relatively few of them have been very active in COA affairs. There are several staff employees who were recruited from among low-income Whites. But, though they outnumber the Black employees, they represent a lower *proportional* representation of their "constituency" than do the Black employees. There are two reasons for this. The Blacks of Sequoyah have responded to the introduction of the COA with greater interest than have Whites of the low-income sector. In addition, there are probably more available Blacks who have adequate qualifications for such staff jobs because the job barrier has prevented Blacks with ability from moving into jobs of this sort in the private sector of the city or county.

Black Youth Groups

A number of Black teen-agers have taken to hanging out in the Neighborhood Center, working as volunteers or just using the facilities provided, such as a TV set and the kitchen. Both boys and girls are included in this group, which forms a loose clique. These young people are somewhat militant. For instance, they have been critical of actions of the older Blacks who are on the Policy Advisory Board of the East Sequoyah Council. They have been especially bitter about a decision by the Board to support a proposed community center to be located in the south end of the city, in Forbes Park. The young people feel that the proposal should have been based on locating the center in the new housing project soon to be built on the grounds of the old Carver School. Their argument is that they need such a center in their own neighborhood. They once spent a whole summer cleaning up the Carver School building on the understanding that they could use it for such a center. Then they were barred from further use of the building by a legal technicality. This was one issue that has had a considerable effect on the militancy.

The Board members supported the Forbes Park location for the proposed community center because they felt that it would be better to have an integrated center. They believed that a center in their own area would tend to be segregated. But the young people are no longer much interested in the issue of desegregation. Rather, they are beginning to be attracted to the idea of separate Black institutions.

The Neighborhood Center clique is probably the most militant of the informal youth groups in the Spout Spring neighborhood. Most others are purely hedonistic in their attitudes. Members of the Neighborhood Center staff have urged the young people in the clique just described to organize all the young people of the Spout Spring neighborhood and then petition for representation on the COA Board of Directors. The COA constitution provides a mandatory procedure for considering such petitions; further, the Board of Directors indicated that it would give such a petition from the young Blacks serious consideration. However, the young people did not, themselves, take the opportunity seriously and, so far, have not made an effort to develop the organization suggested.

Attitudes toward Organizations

The failure of the young people to organize seems to us to exemplify a strong antipathy toward formal organization that is shared by Whites and Blacks of the west Ozarka region. Men seem to be even more anti-organization than women, at least in the Black community of Sequoyah. In that community formal groups without women members simply do not last; but groups with women members do persist. Men generally avoid the responsibility of office-holding and will attend meetings only when strongly persuaded by their wives.

Mr. Tom Welty, president of the Civic Club, and one of the few men who consistently participate in formal organizations, explained his own (and, incidentally, the general feelings of men) on this subject, as follows: "I prefer to have Mrs. Sally Dale, our vice-president, take over a meeting if it is going to get into complications. She knows the rules better 'n I do, and she likes to speak up better than I do. I'm willing to keep this job because we need to get men into this kind of thing more. But, if I think it's getting outside of what I can handle, then it's better for Sally to take over. She'll do a better job of running a meeting of that kind. Most of the men down here won't even go to a meeting if they think it's goin' to be long and if there's going to be a lot of motions, and amendments, and seconding—and all that. The men call that spinning our wheels and they don't think it gets anywhere. Truth is, it doesn't about 90 percent of the time. Or, at least, what gets done don't amount to nothin' considering all the fuss. But that other 10 percent could maybe be important. But most of the men don't see it that way."

The unwillingness of Black men to participate in organizational matters probably represents a reluctance to sacrifice spare time. Leisure is relatively scarce for most men, and they prefer to spend it in more relaxing ways than attending meetings. But women also value their spare time, which is at least as scarce as men's. So there must be some other factor that can explain why some women are willing to accept demanding organizational responsibilities and quite a few women will attend meetings. That other factor seems to be greater facility with the etiquette of organizational activity. Men are ill at ease at meetings. Rules of order and artificial aspects of formal group activity seem silly and time-wasting to them. Many women share their views. But some women, and a few men, do seem to have overcome their anti-organization feelings sufficiently to acquire some familiarity with organizational tactics. These are the people who carry the load of most formal organizations in the community. Apparently they are products of the leadership-training programs sponsored in the churches. More women than men have undergone this sort of training.

We were told that specific programs devoted to leadership skills have been sponsored by regional organizations of the Methodist and Baptist denominations. Since these programs have been integrated for some time, presumably they have similar influence on White participation in formal organization in west Ozarka. We have seen little evidence of such influence among poor Whites of the region. Poor Whites are less likely to be Methodists than to be Baptists. Further, the particular kinds of Baptist churches to which poor Whites belong are probably too independent in orientation to get involved in regional training programs.

Middle- and upper-class Whites of Sequoyah show much sophistication in the intricacies of formal organizations. They appear to belong to a wide variety of religious denominations—including the Methodist church and the more sophisticated sort of Baptist church. However, much of their organizational expertise is probably a by-product of education—especially professional training in law and business. The religious training programs have probably been most influential in preparing middle- and upper-class White women for participation in formal organizations.

7

Leadership

THE DISCUSSION that completed Chapter 6 might give the impression that leadership in the Sequoyah Black community is a monopoly held by a church-trained elite, mostly made up of women. This is not entirely true. Significant aspects of leadership involve action outside the context of formal group meetings, and different leadership strategies and tactics are needed in this outside context. Thus, some individuals who have not had the church-sponsored leadership training have nevertheless exercised leadership from time to time.

Black leadership in Sequoyah is ambiguous. It is not always clear just who is a leader and who is a follower. Roles change with circumstances. Hence leadership is a diversified, diffuse, and elusive phenomenon. In general, these Black people do not easily give themselves and their loyalties into the hands of leaders. If and when they do, they do so tentatively.

White conceptions—more accurately, misconceptions—of the leadership situation in Sequoyah's Black community have had a peculiar effect on that situation. For instance, in several instances segments of the White establishment have identified supposed Black leaders. This is sometimes a "kiss of death" to the leadership aspirations of such individuals. They usually become pseudo-leaders or "leaders without followers," except to the extent that their White sponsors become, in a sense, their followers. However, a few have managed to utilize the opportunities thus presented to them by White sponsorship to develop truly effective leadership. They do so by convincing other Black people that they are taking advantage of the accidental opportunity to achieve useful ends, not merely for themselves but for other Blacks as well.

Types of Leadership

Black leadership in Sequoyah takes several forms. We can utilize the same goal-orientation categories we applied to non-kin groups to distinguish types of leaders, although actual cases usually involve combinations of these types. Regardless of such compromise combinations, we can speak of leaders whose primary orientations are: (1) accommodationist; (2) assimilationist; and, possibly, (3) separatist. Most present leaders are of the first two types. The third type may be just emerging and may be very important in the future.

Accommodationists

Black people are aware that until recently the White community of Sequoyah placed limits on the effectiveness with which any Black person could exercise significant influence or authority. This is one reason why Sequoyah Black people are especially prone to view pretensions or aspirations to leadership with a good deal of initial cynicism. However, within certain spheres of activity where White support or opposition are regarded as irrelevant, some limited but genuine patterns of leadership have long since been accepted. The limits within which such leadership can be exercised are, however, also implicitly or explicitly defined by Whites. Hence such leaders are essentially accommodationists.

Accommodationists accept the limits within which they can operate and try to work effectively within those limits. For this reason such leaders are sometimes regarded as "Uncle Toms" by Black militants, and even by moderates, and some Whites. The label, as a blanket designation, is unfair. Until quite recently this was just about the only effective kind of leadership that could exist in the Sequoyah Black community, given the nature of the White-Black relations and the fact that Whites dominated most of the social institutions.

Because schools and churches were segregated long ago, two categories of Black professional leadership have been well established—teachers and preachers. Both have had a vested interest in the continuation of the separateness of educational and religious institutions. Thus, until recently, Black teachers and preachers tended to accommodate to White-imposed norms in their leadership activities (though their teaching and preaching styles remained distinctive). However, as the segregated nature of the institutions began to be called into question both nationally and locally, teachers and, to some extent, preachers have tended to become more assimilationist in their orientation. It was an assimilationist-oriented Black teacher who was largely responsible for the founding of the Sequoyah Good Neighbor Council twenty years ago.

Present-day teachers seem to be cautiously assimilationist in an accommodating way; that is, they follow professional guidelines within the school system. These guidelines are consistent with the "quiet desegregation" pattern that has characterized integration in Sequoyah for the past fifteen years or more. Ralph Evans, the last principal of the Carver School, moved into the integrated situation as a physical education teacher and assistant coach in a junior high school. He has tended to operate strictly within his professional capacity. Since he is not a Sequoyah native, he may have been especially hesitant to involve himself in leadership within the community. Mrs. Norman, who taught at the Carver School the year before it closed, has also confined herself to a narrowly "professional approach." This was true during the year she taught in the integrated school. It is also true of her work in the Sequoyah Head-Start system, which includes the operation of the Sequoyah Child Care Center. It should be stressed that both of these professionals represent assimilationist tendencies by the very fact of their inclusion and effective work within integrated institutions. They are accommodationist mainly in the caution they show in these institutional contexts. It may be that they are strongly advised by their superiors to avoid getting involved outside the institutional contexts.

Present-day preachers are also cautious. The churches are still segregated; but there are very tentative moves being made toward possible consolidation with White congregations. The preachers tend to be ambivalent about these moves, since such consolidation would probably terminate their jobs, which bring little income but much prestige.

Assimilationists

Assimilationist leaders actively seek to promote full and equal participation by Blacks in the institutions of the city, county, state, and nation. They believe that Blacks can be fully integrated into the pluralistic society of the United States if that society will cooperate in making such integration possible. They are today by far the most important leaders in the Sequoyah Black community.

Quite a few persons have exercised leadership in the assimilationist style during the past few years. Leaders tend to change over a period of time. Certain persons will be very active for a while, then will retire from prominence to take care of personal affairs. A good example of this is Mrs. Lenore Carter, a widow who is about forty-eight years old. Slim and petite, she is one of the most attractive women in the Spout Spring neighborhood. Yet for several years after her husband's death, she remained unmarried because of her driving devotion to civil rights causes. As a member of the Sequoyah Good Neighbor Council, Mrs. Carter played a pioneer role during the period when "quiet desegregation" was being developed as a technique in Sequoyah. On several occasions she was the first, or among the first, to seek service at previously segregated places, such as movie theaters and restaurants. Usually such confrontations were carefully prearranged by the SGNC, in consultation with the managements involved, and were for the most part outwardly undramatic. But inwardly such situations are emotional crises for the persons involved; they involve the deliberate reversal of deeply ingrained behavior. Even if physical safety is not involved, economic security may well be at stake for the person making this first move to change the norms of the larger community.

The effect of such experiences on the personality of a desegregation pioneer can be quite profound. In Mrs. Carter's case it has accentuated the development of already existing tendencies toward militancy. Mrs. Carter could well develop into a separatist leader; she probably will not because she enjoys the company of her White friends in the SGNC and because this is resented by the young militants or potential militants among the younger people of the Black community.

Lenore Carter's militancy is usually expressed in her rather funny, self-kidding style. This has a great deal of charm for Whites who are essentially sympathetic to intregationist goals. When she bursts out, with a smile, at an SGNC meeting with professors and their wives, "Come on everybody, let's plan a riot," they smile in appreciation and even go along with the idea, verbally. They all know (or assume) that Lenore is no more likely to engage in a riot than they are.

However, Mrs. Carter's militancy has not charmed everybody. It has antagonized potential White employers and even some Blacks. Blacks have reacted by being very uncertain in their acceptance of her as a leader.

Mrs. Carter has been active at different times in the affairs of all the assimilationist groups discussed in Chapter 6. She has also been an important church leader. Her most effective leadership was probably in the SGNC desegregation pioneering. But she was also a key person in getting the Birch Avenue Neighborhood Council set up and was, for a while, its chairman. Since the replacement of the Birch Avenue Council by the East Sequoyah Council, she has withdrawn from COA activities and from most other leadership activities. In part this has been because of economic pressures. During her period of greatest leadership activity, she lost a good deal of time, which she probably should have devoted to making a living. She got into debt and had difficulty establishing credit. Her prominence in SGNC desegregation pioneering may have made the credit situation more difficult; that is, this may have been a form of indirect sanctions applied against her. It seems clear that because of resentment by some White employers, she lost job opportunities during her period of active leadership. On the other hand, her White friends would make up for this by giving her clean-up jobs in their homes. Despite this she is one of the few Black adults in the community who has been unemployed for more than just a few days every year.

Mrs. Carter finally had to remove herself from all but church activities and concentrate on rehabilitating herself financially. She took a business-training course in the COA-sponsored vocational education program during the past year. After completing this training, she obtained a job as receptionist in a business firm managed by a fellow member of the SGNC.

Mrs. Carter's sister, Daphne Newton, has also been a pioneer in desegregation and an important leader in several groups. But her reaction to the emotional strain of this experience has been quite different from Lenore's. She has become increasingly nonmilitant, facing the world with compassion and composure. This may be a continuation of a family tradition of deep religious conviction and devotion to religious service. Yet, from the same family background, Lenore Carter drew the strength to be a dedicated militant.

Mrs. Newton eased herself out of active leadership earlier than did her sister. Several years ago she took advantage of an opportunity to enter training as a practical nurse. After completing this training, she went to work for the COA, and by so doing, brought herself back into leadership, first as a field worker and later as an office worker and semi-administrator. At different times she operates as an organizer or as a practical nurse, depending on the current needs of the organization.

The most spectacular Black leadership career in recent years had been that of Joe Carter. Joe spent a good deal of his early years outside of Sequoyah. This began when he went to Kansas City to attend high school in the late 1940s. He starred as a football player there and later went to college for two years on an athletic scholarship. After that he had a checkered career in different parts of the country. He served an enlistment in the Air Force, worked as a chef in Kansas City and Dallas, and was a playground instructor in Tulsa. Then, in 1963, he returned to Sequoyah and got a job in the shipping department of an electrical supply firm, which had just been established in the city. He was the first Negro hired by this company.

In 1966 Joe accepted an offer to be the assistant director of the Sequoyah Neighborhood Center set up by the newly organized COA. This involved taking a pay reduction, as he was making rather good money at the electrical company by then. At first, Joe worked with a White woman who was the first director of the center. A clash of personalities between them ended in her resignation. Later she became a leader of the dissident liberals who attacked the COA administration in 1967 and 1968.

Joe's comment to us concerning his former colleague in the center reveals certain problems in the relations between White liberals and Blacks. "Mrs. Perkins was a real democratic lady," he said. "But she knew what was best for the Black people. So her idea of community action was to have us democratically support all of her ideas. And if we didn't always do this, she got mighty upset about it. But she didn't hold a grudge. She was nice enough to ask me if my wife would work for her as a housekeeper, so she could have time enough for this job of helping us poor people out of our poverty. She's gone on to another city now and I understand she's a pretty big wheel in a Head-Start program there. Actually she had good ideas, especially on how to help kids. I gave her pretty much of a hard time and I kind of regret it now. But it seemed like I had to stand up for the independence of the Blacks—for our right to do our own thinking and even make our own mistakes."

Joe Carter became the Director of the Neighborhood Center after the resignation of Mrs. Perkins. In this work he has had a number of outstanding successes but also some disappointing failures. His biggest success was probably the organization of a tutoring program for low-income children in the Sequoyah schools. This program depended heavily on recruitment of OSU students as tutors, and Mr. Carter turned out to be very persuasive in recruiting these tutors. He was so persuasive that he was placed in charge of developing a tutoring program for the entire county; it was felt that his influence on the college students would be the key to success for this expanded program.

Joe Carter has also been very successful in organizing fund-raising dinners for various causes in the Black community. In these efforts he has always been strongly supported by the Civic Club. Within the Black community he was, for a time, very influential in organizing teen-agers to carry out projects in connection with the COA. Initially his personal influence with these young people was very great; but it began to deteriorate after the humiliating failure of the Carver School project. Aided by OSU students and some White teen-agers, the young people worked very hard to clean up the old school in preparation for its use as a community center. They succeeded in fixing it up in a very ingenious way. After completing their work, they were able to have one or two record dances in the building. Then, because of concern about insurance liability, the Sequoyah School Board decided to withdraw their permission to use the building. This had a very disillusioning effect on the young people and drastically reduced Joe Carter's prestige. He had come to be a person who could get results from White people, but, after the Carver School withdrawal, he seemed to be a person who could not be trusted. After the young people were barred from the school building they turned their anger against the building, breaking every window in it.

Joe Carter's main weakness in his COA job involved certain aspects of administration. He was a good idea man. He could think up projects and he could get them going. But he was very casual about paper work. In the early days of the agency, this was not serious. But as the agency became established as a bureaucratic organization, with a good deal of federal money to spend, the need to keep adequate records and make frequent and detailed reports of daily activities was increasingly emphasized. Carter became the despair of the higher administration, which had somehow to fill out his reports for him. Finally they solved the problem by hiring an assistant for him and placing her in charge of doing all his paper work. This girl has her troubles keeping up with what Joe is doing. At least once a week she threatens to resign. But, as long as she stays with the job, the paper work will probably get done.

The most interesting thing about Joe Carter's leadership is his style, which is a kind of caricature of the typical Black militant urban ghetto leader. Joe wears clothing symbolic of Black power, and he wears his hair "natural." His conversation is peppered with Black Power slogans and expressions, delivered with a twinkle in his eye. Although COA officials despair of his casual administrative habits, he is extremely popular with them and with all his co-workers in the agency. He is a hard worker and is especially good at helping other COA directors in emergency situations.

Although he caricatures the Black militant and has several times told us that he regarded the assimilationist approach as the only effective one to use in Sequoyah, Joe Carter is definitely attracted to the values and symbols of the national mood of Black militancy. With his great physical strength and his charismatic personality he could quite possibly have had a successful leadership career in the ghettos.

Thus, in a sense, Joe Carter plays a separatist role as well as an assimilationist one. This has especially applied to his influence on young Black boys and girls, for he has certainly produced separatist tendencies in them. One or two of these young people have shown some potential for leadership. This may be more effectively expressed in the future, but at present their militance has been chiefly verbal and confused.

What we have attempted in this section on leadership has been to show tendencies in terms of selected examples. We wish to enter, here, a word of caution. Our examples have been selected mainly on the basis of our own personal familiarity with the persons involved and their careers. We do not imply that these are the only leaders—or even the most important ones. There are others whose activities have been less dramatic but perhaps more effective. The many quiet church-trained leaders who keep formal groups going and the men who led the way through the job barrier during the 1950s are certainly as important as the flamboyant Joe Carter.

8

Culture

AS ANTHROPOLOGISTS STUDYING THE SEQUOYAH BLACK COMMUNITY, we
have looked for cultural similarities in behavior, possessions, and attitudes. We have found considerable diversity. Black people of Sequoyah
do not live alike or think alike. They buy different kinds of clothing, different
kinds of cars. There are other marked variations in behavior and attitudes, although
there are some unifying tendencies as well. We find the degree of diversity dis-
concerting since, as anthropologists, we are trained to expect cultural homogeneity
in a small community. To us the degree of diversity in *this* small community
reflects the range of cultural variation one expects in a much larger community;
and in a sense, this is the case. We have concluded that the diversity in the Spout
Spring neighborhood is an expression of certain cultural themes, which are characteristic of the whole west Ozarka region.

Subcultural Themes

Cultural *themes* are a series of statements that summarize important
tendencies in behavior, attitudes, and values found to be expressed in a particular
society (Opler 1945). The lifeways of western Ozarka are simply a special version
of the general culture of the United States. Therefore, we speak of *subcultural
themes* in our attempt to state the distinctive tendencies we find in the behavior,
attitudes, and values of people in this part of this state.

Several of the Ozarka themes we suggest are expressions of a tendency
toward nonconformity; some are, indeed, negative themes, which express specific
conformity-avoidance with respect to certain types of life situations. Though we
have derived these themes from observations throughout west Ozarka, we find
that they apply to the Black population of Sequoyah about as well as they do to
the White population of the area.

The themes we propose for the west Ozarka subculture are discussed in
the following sections.

1. ANTI-ORGANIZATION THEME   People tend to avoid commitment to group action, especially if the group involves formal organization. Families and churches are exceptions to this theme.

2. ANTI-STRANGERS THEME   People tend to avoid contact with outsiders or to exhibit considerable reserve toward them, at least until such outsiders have been sized up by all members of a family, clique, or community. This theme is sometimes expressed in hostile action but, basically, it is one of caution and noninvolvement.

3. ANTI-LEADER THEME   People tend to reject leadership aspirations by in-group members, especially if these aspirations are unexpected and involve moves toward organization or change. This often results in the phenomenon of "leaders without followers."

4. ANTI-GOVERNMENT THEME   People tend to be cynical about government at all levels. They resent the extension of governmental authority over their lives. They accept government programs that benefit their area (such as a series of dams and reservoirs along the Elk River) but resent the increased federal presence these programs imply. Similarly they participate in the processes of local and state government but seek to curb the power and effectiveness of these governmental levels.

5. MORALITY-OF-CRITICISM THEME   People seem to feel a moral imperative to be critical; that is, they have a compulsion to express criticism rather than to suppress it, if it is felt that criticism is justified.

6. TAKE-CARE-OF-YOUR-OWN THEME   People have a strong basic loyalty to relatives and friends. This applies even if they criticize them, in terms of Theme 5. Such criticism will usually be verbal; loyalty will be expressed in actual support behavior when needed.

7. MALE-FEMALE ANTAGONISM THEME   People tend to see the male role in terms of exaggerated masculine dominance in sexual behavior and in family relations. This is especially characteristic of male attitudes and actions but is also frequently expressed in female expectations. At the same time, there is a tendency to see certain aspects of male chauvinism as morally bad—laziness, exploitation of women's labor, sexual exploitation of women, and meanness toward wives and children. This is most frequently expressed by women in criticism of men but is also often expressed in male attitudes about other men. As a general result there are certain stereotypes of hostile expression between men and women. These are frequently disguised as "kidding" and are the raw material for much humor.

8. BLACK-HUMOR THEME   People have a strong tendency to see humor in misfortune and tragedy, probably as an attempt to ease these situations. They readily express this verbally. The misfortune involved may be one's own or somebody else's.

9. STERN-GOD THEME   People are, for the most part, either strongly fundamentalist in their religion, or hedonistically defiant of the fundamentalist restrictions on behavior. The dominant Protestant sects or denominations of the region stress the touchy, vengeful, Old Testament God, rather than the tolerant, loving God of the New Testament.

10. PERSONAL-AUTONOMY THEME   People tend to be rugged individualists in fact as well as in theory. Individuals often assert their personalities in an ag-

gressive, even violent, manner. They assert their individualism also in strong insistence on private property rights, property acquisition, and litigatious attitudes about personal rights. However, individualism is sometimes expressed in subtle, less aggressive ways. The main point is that personality is somehow expressed in a recognizably distinct manner.

Implications of the Themes

Theme 10 seems to be very basic, finding expression in many of the others. It certainly underlies the four negative themes, as well as certain aspects of Themes 5 and 8 (Morality of Criticism and Black Humor). However, not all of the themes are completely nonconformist in their implications. Themes 5, 6, 7, 8, and 9 (Morality of Criticism, Take Care of Your Own, Male-Female Antagonism, Black Humor, and Stern God) certainly suggest some behavioral and attitudinal consistencies. This is true even of typical manifestations of the negative themes and of Theme 10 (Personal Autonomy).

Black Expression of the Themes

Modes of conformity and nonconformity in the Sequoyah Black community seem to be generally consistent with Ozarka modes of conformity and nonconformity, as expressed in our list of themes. We recognize that these do not tell the whole story. For instance, job barriers and other subtle or nonsubtle restrictions on behavior produce special problems, and special solutions to these problems, for Black people here as they do for Blacks throughout the United States. Personal deviations from all these themes can be noted. It is especially necessary to single out four significant ways in which the behavior of Sequoyah Black people varies from that of most Whites native to the region. These variations concern Themes 2, 4, 9, and 10.

With respect to Theme 2 (Anti-Strangers), we must point out that attitudes toward strangers have not noticeably handicapped us in our work in the Sequoyah Black community. We did undergo some preliminary sizing up but very quickly found ourselves enjoying excellent relations with most people in all walks of life. There are a few Black people who always maintained great reserve toward us, were wary of any contact with us, and preferred not to get into discussions with us. So, our experiences certainly did not disprove the theme. But we can say that we found it somewhat easier to get to know members of the Black community than native White people in west Ozarka. Among these Whites we do have many friends, but Whites generally seem to have more reserve, more barriers that are never fully penetrated by strangers, than do Blacks.

With respect to Theme 4 (Anti-Government), we found that Black people of Sequoyah are well aware of the important role the federal government plays in providing and upgrading opportunities for Black people. However, they are usually skeptical about specific programs until they find that these really have some effect for them. They feel that some programs are of no practical use to them. For example, they value highly the Sequoyah Child Care Center, which was set up in Sequoyah late in 1967 by the federally funded COA; but they have been quite critical of many details of its organization and administration. Most Sequoyah Black people see no value in urban-renewal programs; indeed many fear that urban renewal in Sequoyah might cause them to lose homes they now own.

We found Theme 9 (Stern God) to be present but not dominant in the Black community. Except for the Church of Christ, the congregations do not generally apply official doctrine very strictly. In practice there is considerable tolerance of hedonistic deviations from strict behavioral norms. By way of contrast, hedonism among native Whites involves a hard choice: You either fear the Lord or you defy him. Black hedonism is pleasure that the Lord will understand and, if necessary, will be ready to forgive.

Theme 10 (Personal Autonomy) holds true of Blacks as well as Whites. However, most Blacks express their personalities in relatively subtle ways. There is less direct aggressiveness among Black people than among Whites. Aggressiveness in the personalities of some Blacks seems to run in certain families, and it is generally increasing among young people. From time to time there are some very direct and violent expressions of this between men in Grant's Place. But Grant usually gets the participants outside before a fight starts.

We must point out that there are some important outside cultural influences at work in Sequoyah and in the rest of west Ozarka that are affecting all segments of the nation's people. Television and the other media of mass communications are perhaps the strongest of these influences. They certainly tend to encourage modes of mass conformity that are nationwide. It is also noteworthy that Ozarka State University brings in diverse people and ideas. The norms of modern business practice tend toward a bland kind of conformity and agreeableness in relations between sales people and customers. The phenomenon of "pseudo-gemeinschaft" (insincere or unrealistic sociability) is certainly present. All of these influences must be taken into consideration in connection with contemporary lifeways in west Ozarka.

Nevertheless, the old way of life persists. For instance, individualism of a self-assertive type often emerges triumphant over "pseudo-gemeinschaft" in the behavior of businessmen and sales people, especially in locally owned business establishments. Since outside influences brought in through the university tend more toward diversity than toward conformity, they actually enrich some of the themes, especially Theme 10 (Personal Autonomy).

Since most of the native population of western Ozarka is White and of "old Anglo-Saxon stock," it may seem odd that the Negroes of Sequoyah share the west Ozarka subculture. There is certainly no strong consciousness of similarity on the part of either the White mountaineer or the Black townsman. Young Black people indignantly deny any similarity: "You're sayin' we're like that old man with the mule!" (This is probably a reference to the comic-strip character Snuffy Smith and his mule Aunt Sukie.)

However, it must be remembered that culture is a social inheritance, not a biological inheritance. That is, it is *learned*. Such learning is through example and

Older house of basic four-room type in The Valley. Note the stone foundation and steps.

symbolic communication with others. The learning process is a very subtle and devious one—more an unconscious process than a deliberate one. Most Black families in Sequoyah have roots in west Ozarka; in many cases these go back more than a hundred years. It is not strange that they have acquired behavior patterns that express west Ozarka themes. Because of the small size of the Black population, interaction with the White people of the area has always been close and intense. We feel that this has been a very important factor in developing and maintaining ties between Sequoyah Blacks and the subculture of their region.

We will now turn to a consideration of certain aspects of culture in the Sequoyah Black community, which have not been dealt with before—or which we wish to restate for emphasis. We have, of course, already dealt in other chapters with many aspects of culture. Social organization has been more emphasized than other aspects, thus far. In the remainder of this chapter, we shall deal with the following topics: (1) material culture, the "artifacts" people own and use; (2) entertainment; and (3) values and beliefs.

Possessions

The material culture of the Sequoyah Black community is, for the most part, simply an expression of the general material culture of the United States. There are no classes of artifacts used or owned by these people that differ from comparable classes of artifacts used or owned by other people in the nation. The particular models of automobiles owned by Black people here do not differ significantly, if at all, from similar models of such cars owned by other people in Sequoyah or elsewhere in the United States. The same principle applies to houses, furniture, clothing, foods, and tools. It is of course true that it is economically impossible or impractical for Black people of Sequoyah to use or own certain other artifacts, simply because they lack the money to buy them. But this same limitation applies to other poor people in Sequoyah and elsewhere in the nation.

Housing

Houses in Spout Spring are similar to houses in other parts of Sequoyah occupied by predominantly low-income families. The characteristics of these houses are especially similar to the characteristics of houses owned by low-income Whites with respect to age, size, condition, and structural materials. However, so far as location is concerned, there is a characteristic that is unique to Negroes— namely, segregation. Negro housing is largely limited to those houses available in the Spout Spring neighborhood, as described and delimited in Chapter 2. However, the houses of poor Whites also tend to cluster in certain neighborhoods of Sequoyah. Some of these neighborhoods adjoin the Spout Spring neighborhood and are included with it in the Birch Avenue Target Area defined by the County Outreach Agency. There are more White families than Black families in this target area. Their houses are essentially similar to those of the Blacks.

Recently remodeled house in The Flat.

The southern portion of the Spout Spring neighborhood, known as "the Flat," is actually an area of mixed White and Black residences. The families there, both Black and White, can be described as lower-middle class. Their houses are neat, well-kept though modest dwellings.

Our count revealed 120 separate residential structures in the Spout Spring neighborhood. In addition, there are three church buildings, one abandoned school building, one community clubhouse, and one beer tavern. Ten of the residential structures that were unoccupied at the time of our study have since been condemned and torn down. Roughly two-thirds of the remaining 110 houses are owned by their occupants. Most of them are single-story, single-family dwellings. Buildings vary with respect to size, age, structural materials, and state of repair; but they are mostly small, wooden, gabled structures with a living room, bathroom, kitchen, two small bedrooms, and an attic under the gabled roof. House foundations are usually of substantial field or quary stone, well mortared, and so constructed as to level the house on a sloping lot. Most houses are between forty and sixty years old.

The city's planning consultant has classified two-thirds of the Black-occupied houses as deteriorating or dilapidated. Essentially our survey agrees. However, many houses in the "deteriorating" category may still be rehabilitated and in many cases Black families are attempting such rehabilitation. Most Blacks who own their homes would prefer to keep them rather than accept the alternative of renting in new public housing projects. They are seriously disturbed about the possibility of a sweeping urban-renewal project.

About eighty of the occupied houses in the Black residential area fit, in a general way, the description just given, although there are considerable variations in neatness and in basic structural conditions. About thirty of the occupied dwellings vary more definitely from the general type just described. Fifteen of these are small structures in rather bad states of repair. The other fifteen are more pretentious than the basic type in size or condition or both. Some of these relatively high-quality houses are quite old; but most of them have been built within the last ten to twenty years, and some newer ones are constructed of stone or concrete blocks rather than wood.

The better houses vary in style and furnishings. All show attention to structural excellence, have quality furniture (old or new), and provide a sense of creature comfort. It is noteworthy that the owners of such houses generally have high incomes, comparatively speaking, and show considerable skill in planning and income management. Others with comparable incomes have houses of the basic type described above. In some cases, these houses, too, are well built and structurally sound; but they are usually less orderly and not as well planned and managed. In general, the most important reason for this seems to be family size. Large families mean wear and tear on furniture, interest in other forms of self-expression than housing and housekeeping, and too little time for work around the house. At all levels of income there are families that are simply too large for the houses they occupy.

Extremely large families are rare today. However, we have record of thirty families in the Spout Spring neighborhood with between five and twelve members. On the other hand, there are enough people living in one- or two-person households to bring the average household size down to around 3.8 persons. There are a few houses with two or more families (or independent individuals) living in them; hence the number of household (117) exceeds the number of occupied houses (110).

Furnishings

Variations in taste are expressed in a wide range of furniture types, representing different time periods over the last hundred years. Relatively recent overstuffed styles are more frequently encountered than others. Interesting variations from this norm involve both the old and the new. There are a few families owning elegant, old-fashioned furniture that has been in the family for two or more generations. There are also a few families that favor modern furniture that is spare in style and simple in line.

Most homes have television sets, and a surprisingly high number of them are color sets. These are a considerable expense, not only because of their high original cost but because a cable hook-up is necessary in Sequoyah, where the mountain terrain around the city effectively blocks direct reception of outside television channels. Installation and usage fees must be paid for the hook-up. Other types of appliances found in most Black homes are those typical of most Sequoyah residences: refrigerators; stoves; electric coffee makers, can openers, and mixers; heaters, both gas and electric; and telephones.

Clothing

Most Black people in Sequoyah spend relatively little money on clothes, as compared to food, appliances, and cars. In general, they own at least one "dress-up" outfit, which usually means a suit for the men and a good dress with hat for the women. Teen-agers probably spend more on clothing than adults do and usually have more colorful tastes than adults, who are generally rather conservative. Working clothes are simple, neat, and inexpensive. Most men wear work clothes even during leisure time, as do most low-income White men in the city and county. We know of only two Black men who have unusually expensive wardrobes and who are rarely seen in work clothes when not at their places of employment.

There is a recent trend for young people to adopt items of dress that are symbolically African. These are essentially supplementary to the basic clothing that is available in Sequoyah stores or through mail-order houses. It is interesting that Blacks seem more skillful than the majority of Whites in the city at developing individual styling possibilities in conventional clothing. This is especially true of women and of teen-agers of both sexes.

Cars

Most Black families have cars, often two or more. These are usually fairly recent models, large, light-colored, and in the medium-price range. A few very expensive, late-model cars are also to be seen. On the other hand, there are some jalopies. Most cars are being purchased on long-term credit through installment buying, as are many of the other possessions mentioned earlier. Cars are usually a necessity for employment, since Sequoyah has no public transportation system and the majority of jobs are located some distance from the Black residential area. Since, typically, both husband and wife work (in different places), the need for separate cars is quite real. If a person does not have a car, or if it is being repaired, he may have to take a taxi to work. Taxis are not cheap but are often used, out of sheer necessity. Some employers pay taxi fares for their domestic help, in addition to their basic pay.

Entertainment

Recreation, for Black people of Sequoyah, involves the various mass media to a very considerable extent. Yet there is also much individual self-expression shown in pleasurable activities. The mass media most frequently used are TV

Family get-together in The Valley.

and motion pictures. General magazines, picture magazines, sports magazines, fashion magazines, movie magazines, phonograph records, and newspapers are also important, in about that order. (Comic books, surprisingly, are not especially popular.) The favorite TV programs and movies seem to reflect the general national preferences, with westerns and law-enforcement themes ranking high. Until recently the participation of Black performers did not influence choice of programs or movies to a noticeable extent. But this is changing, now that TV and the movies increasingly cast Black performers in important and unstereotyped roles and give emphasis to Black singers and singing groups. Probably Black selectivity applies more strongly to the choice of phonograph records and picture magazines. The standard picture magazines, *Life* and *Look*, are popular; but *Ebony*, the Black-oriented picture magazine, is more popular than both the others combined. Soul music records are popular on the juke box at Grant's Place and in personal collections. All young people claim to have record players, and home use of phonographs is important, despite the competition of television for listening time. Transistor radios are very popular and are used mainly for listening to music.

Drinking

Most men and some women drink alcoholic beverages regularly. Among hard liquors, expensive scotch and bourbon whiskeys are preferred. But Black people probably drink more beer than hard liquor. This reflects both comparative costs and the legal norms of Ozarka. The sale of liquor by the drink is illegal in the state, though the law is circumvented by Whites through the institution of the private club. On the other hand, beer can be sold by the drink in licensed taverns. Negroes have no difficulty buying whiskey or other spirits at liquor stores. But the large amount of social drinking at Grant's, which can legally only involve beer, probably tips the scales quantitatively toward a greater amount of beer-drinking. Grant does not serve liquor illegally; his license is too valuable to risk.

"If a cat brings in a pint and sips it quietly at his table, I don't mind," says Grant. "But, man, if they start passing that stuff around too much, I stop it. Fuzz drops in here every evening and the's no use throwing that in their face. Besides, I got to sell beer to pay the rent."

Liquor is consumed at parties, in cars, or at home. A good many parties in Sequoyah are mixed, a very recent development. Certain of the young people and even a fair number of older men and women of the Black community drop in on parties at the homes of professors and students. Native Whites are less likely to have Black guests at their parties, but they do not necessarily react with shock to find Blacks at parties to which they have been invited by professors or students. This reflects the current fact that Blacks are "in" if they are interesting. Therefore, the more militant Blacks are the most coveted guests at such parties, and some Sequoyah Blacks who are not really very militant have learned to put on at least a good militant act—usually with tongue in cheek. Joe Carter is perhaps the most accomplished parlor militant in Sequoyah, but there are others. In the "swinging circuit," Grant Barbour is the most popular Black. He is not a militant and does not pretend to be; but he is a charming hedonist.

Music and Dance

Present-day self-expression in dancing and singing shows some interesting contrasts. Religious sanctions against dancing are strong. But religion is quite permissive toward singing, so much so, that one of the most important outlets for song is the church service. We feel that music is the most important link tying Sequoyah Blacks to a national Black subculture. Their singing is not a part of the regional subculture. Its distinctiveness is clearly expressed in the soul music of small singing groups and in the singing of hymns. Singing in Black churches is characterized by the use of lining and response. The preacher, who is often the lead singer, sings a line of the hymn; then the congregation repeats it. The distinctive thing about the singing in Black churches is the complexity of the rhythm, especially in the responses. Some White churches in west Ozarka that don't permit the use of musical instruments utilize this technique, but the quality isn't the same; the response singing there is straightforward and simple, essentially repetition of the preacher's lead.

Dancing is officially forbidden by the Church of Christ and is frowned upon by the other two churches. Despite these negative attitudes, dance finds expression. People dance informally at home or at Grant's. They dance more formally at parties and at dances held on certain days at a recently integrated skating rink on the south edge of town. Record dances are popular whenever a place can be found in which to hold them. Joe Carter sponsored such dances in the Carver School building and later in the Civic Club building.

The interest of young White students and professors' families in the Black subculture is especially focused on music. Therefore, the biracial parties that have become popular emphasize informal singing and dancing in the Black style. The records of popular Black performers are especially prized at such affairs.

Today, there are few Black instrumentalists in Sequoyah. The only "professional" we know is Bobby Cummings, a handyman in an apartment complex who moonlights as a jazz drummer evenings and weekends. Several women are accomplished pianists but perform only in churches or at parties. There is one piano teacher; her style is classical, not jazz or blues.

Sports

Sequoyah Blacks are much interested in sports, both as spectators and participants. Boys participate enthusiastically in Little League and American Legion baseball as members of carefully integrated teams. In general, they are capable players, and several of them have, in recent years, been stars of their teams. A similarly organized football league for younger boys has recently been set up, and it also features carefully integrated teams. Games are well attended by the parents and relatives of the players, as well as by others.

When Sequoyah High School was first integrated, in 1954, one of the results was the first undefeated team in the school's history. The star fullback of this team, Steve Johnson, was the first Negro to play for SHS. Since then other Negro athletes have performed on the football, basketball, baseball, and track teams of Sequoyah High School, although none have made the teams very recently.

No Negroes played for Ozarka State University teams until the winter of 1967–1968, when there was one Black on the basketball squad. He was not a local boy. The athletic department at the university has a reputation among other faculty members of being strongly segregationist. This has not dampened the ardor of Black people for OSU teams, especially for the football team, which has been very successful in recent years. The football team is an almost sacred institution in Sequoyah and throughout the state. It appears to be as strongly supported by Blacks as by Whites.

However, the segregationist attitude attributed to the OSU athletic department has seriously affected the attitude of Sequoyah Black youth toward the university as an institution. They tend to feel that they are "not wanted up there." As a matter of fact, this is far from the truth. Except for some old-timers, the faculty members are sympathetic and integrationist in their attitudes. But the young people see the university largely in terms of athletics, as do most young people throughout the state. Therefore, a majority of the local Black youth who go to college go elsewhere. This has been especially true of athletes. Unable to get scholarships at OSU, they have gone to other schools in the state and have been welcomed, even in schools that were "lily-white" less than ten years ago. In 1968 four young men from the Sequoyah Black community had athletic scholarships and were playing for teams of schools in other parts of Ozarka.

Drugs

We have conflicting reports concerning drug use among Black people in Sequoyah. There is considerable use of marijuana and LSD reported among White students at the university. A number of White students tell us that drug use is also widespread among young Blacks in Sequoyah and that some older persons also use drugs. Black young people with whom we have discussed this matter deny the allegation indignantly. They claim that only a few people in their community use drugs. Newspaper accounts of police raids in which people are arrested with drugs in their possession usually involve Whites rather than Blacks. One exception, however, was the arrest of a young man who was especially vehement in denying to us the importance of drug use in the Black community. A prominent Black leader has been identified to us as the principal supplier of marijuana in the community; but the same person is also cited as being responsible for influencing young teen-agers away from drug use.

Values and Beliefs

When we discussed values at the beginning of this chapter, our primary concern was to outline the cultural similarity of Whites and Blacks in west Ozarka in terms of our ten proposed themes. In these concluding sections we take a more detailed look at the values and beliefs of Black people. We see four basic value orientations in the Sequoyah Black community. One is a form of the Protestant ethic. Another, in sharp contrast, is a form of hedonism that places high value on the attainment of pleasure. A third value orientation is a gentler and more tolerant version of Christianity than the Protestant ethic. A fourth basic value, Negritude, may be in the process of establishing itself.

Protestant Ethic, Hedonism, and Christianity

All three of the Black churches in Sequoyah are Protestant. All three represent denominations that are well established in the west Ozarka region. The Baptists and Methodists are indeed among the principal Protestant denominations in the United States, ranking second and third among the nation's churches (Ogburn and Nimkoff 1964: 590, Table 40). The Church of Christ is less important nationally but is very important in the state of Ozarka.

Locally the most fundamentalist of the three churches is the Church of Christ, which stresses a very literal interpretation of the Bible and its relevance to all aspects of life. This is the newest church in the Black community, having been founded in 1962. Although still the smallest of the three chruches, so far as local membership is concerned, it appears to be the most dynamic, judging by attendance and general participation. Brother Graham Shaw, the Church of Christ preacher, is a spirited and inspiring leader, whose congregation obviously responds to his preaching with great sincerity. The other two churches have basically fundamentalist traditions, but these are not especially stressed today. The Methodist minister, Reverend J. L. Allen, does have a wonderfully emotional fundamentalist style; but his congregation does not reflect this style ideologically. The former Baptist minister preached in a lower key than either Brother Shaw or Reverend Allen, expressing fundamentalism but not emphasizing it.

The Church of Christ membership has grown at the expense of the other two churches, but it has recruited more from the Methodists than from the Baptists. In general, it seems to represent a resurgence of fundamentalism as a vital force in the community. This is associated with a strong rejection of Negritude and Black Power. Hard work, a virtuous life, fear of God, and active participation in the Church of Christ (conceptualized as literally the only true church) are stressed as the proper means of bettering one's lot.

Although fundamentalism and the sterner aspect of God are played down at the Baptist church and arouse no strong congregational enthusiasm at the Methodist church, they still are incorporated to some extent in religious instruction in both churches. Thus, the Protestant Ethic is not confined entirely to the Church of Christ, although it is doubtless strongest there. A hedonistic orientation is also important among some members of the older churches, as well as among those few Blacks with no church affiliation. But the value orientation that seems most prominent in the older churches is a kind of synthesis of Christianity with hedonism. Most members of the older churches seem to interpret Christianity in this sense, seeing God as a gentle and loving personage who is rather tolerant of pleasure-seeking. Pure hedonism, without any concern for God, probably occurs rarely among Sequoyah Blacks. But as an element in the over-all value system, hedonism is most important, not only because of its presence in the gentler version of Christianity just described but also because it crops up, ambivalently, in the behavior of many whose dominant value orientation is the Protestant Ethic.

Negritude

We have several times referred to Negritude in this chapter. By Negritude we refer to a value orientation that emphasizes the importance of being Negro, both biologically and culturally. We recognize that the term is not often used today in the United States, owing to the current antipathy to the term "Negro" among Blacks and their White sympathizers. However, we know of no convenient comparable term utilizing the more popular "Black," although the slogan "Black is beautiful" expresses the thought.

Until quite recently we did not consider Negritude to be a significant factor in the value orientation of Sequoyah Negroes. The small size and relative isolation of this Black community seemed to explain the absence of Negritude. We therefore felt that the traditional cultural orientation was not favorable to its development.

Today, we find the situation is changing. Negritude is emerging as a potentially significant factor among the young people of Sequoyah. This is so new a development that we were not aware of it when we began to work on this book. A mild civil rights sentiment had long existed in Sequoyah, mainly expressed in the biracial Sequoyah Good Neighbor Council. A process of "quiet desegregation" had been fostered by this organization, paralleling changes elsewhere in the nation. Nonlocal Black students at the university sometimes voiced more militant sentiments than those expressed by the SGNC. But only in 1968 did we find Negritude surfacing as a value clearly expressed in the behavior and attitudes of a number of local Black people. There is some possiblity that this is a specific reaction to the assassination of Dr. Martin Luther King in Memphis that spring. One Black teen-ager from Sequoyah attended the funeral of Dr. King. After he returned from the funeral he seemed to have become an articulate Black militant. However, other young Black people state that throughout 1967 they had been increasingly aware of the doctrine being preached by such national Black Power leaders as Stokely Carmichael and H. Rapp Brown.

Some young adults, as well as most teen-agers, appear to be attracted to

Negritude. Older people are for the most part either indifferent or hostile. We cannot venture to predict what future Negritude may have in west Ozarka, but it seems unlikely to thrive in a region with so few Blacks. On the other hand, the concept has surprisingly strong popularity among many, young Whites, especially at the university, and this may guarantee it a future.

9

Change

S EQUOYAH HAS NEVER BEEN A QUIET CULTURAL BACKWATER despite its location in a mountainous corner of the state of Ozarka. Many rural portions of Lincoln County have been quite isolated in the past; some are relatively isolated even today. But the more populous areas of the county have always been accessible. Hence change has been a continuous influence on most of the county's population, though its impact has usually been more immediate and intense in Sequoyah, the economic, political, and communications center. Cultural change has also affected the Sequoyah Black community, as well as the other Black people in Lincoln County, but it has often been different in kind and in degree from the change that has affected the White population. The reason for this is that change has often been selectively screened by Whites, who controlled the very institutions it has threatened.

Today, changes in the culture of the Black community of Sequoyah are going on at a somewhat accelerated pace. Although Whites are still involved in the process of change, they no longer completely control it. The main purpose of this chapter is to analyze this recent period of cultural change. However, we will first present a brief summary of changes that have taken place in the past.

1830–1945

The earliest settlers in Lincoln County included Blacks as well as Whites. Blacks who came into the county between 1830 and 1860 were mostly slaves, though a few "freemen of color" are listed in the 1840, 1850, and 1860 censuses. Black settlement, like White settlement, was mostly rural, since a majority of the Negroes were agricultural laborers, "field hands." However, the town of Sequoyah always had a small but significant Black component in its population: house servants, artisans, and unskilled labor. Skilled Negro artisans, both slave and free, were employed in furniture-making, brick-making, smithing, and construction work (according to White persons of old pioneer families we have interviewed). The Black population of the county reached a peak of over 1500 in 1860, constituting about one-tenth of the total population of the county.

The Civil War brought dramatic changes to Lincoln County. Bands of armed men roamed over the land, and life became unpredictable and dangerous. After the War, emancipation brought problems of adjustment and survival. By 1870 the Black population of the county had dropped to less than 700, a loss of over 50 percent in ten years. Emigration probably accounted for much of this loss, but there are traditional accounts that suggest a high death rate due to starvation or sickness among Blacks of the county between 1860 and 1870. Sequoyah may have been a relatively safe refuge for some families during this period. In any case, the Black population of the town increased about one-third during the 1860–1870 decade.

The growth of Sequoyah during the last three decades of the nineteenth century was marked by sufficient prosperity to ensure the presence of many middle- and upper-class White families, whose service needs provided employment for the growing Black population of the town. Negro families were scattered throughout the town rather than concentrated in one place. Most Negro families lived close to the White families for whom they worked.

Negroes who remained in rural parts of the county became a kind of rural proletariat, working as sharecroppers or as wage-laborers in agriculture. There were also some Black landowners, who were independent farmers on a small scale. In the small towns of the county, there were some Negroes working as servants, laborers, or artisans.

It is not clear just when the concentration of Negro settlement in the Spout Spring district first began. We have heard conflicting statements on this point from both Blacks and Whites. The city's planning consultant has recently stated that the Spout Spring district of Sequoyah has been a Negro residential area ever since the Civil War. But we have been told by both Blacks and Whites that there have been corn fields in the valley of Forbes Branch and on the lower slopes rising out of it within the century. Quite possibly a few Negro families lived in the area during the late nineteenth century and engaged in truck gardening or small-scale farming. More intensive settlement probably began soon after 1900. By the 1920s the Spout Spring district had a population of about 200. Most Black families now living in the area seem to have moved in from rural parts of the county within the last two or three generations. Today, only three Black persons in the county live outside Sequoyah.

Until recently Negro employment in Sequoyah mainly involved domestic service, food preparation, clean-up work, and general unskilled labor. Job lists for men and women, which we have abstracted from the 1935 Sequoyah City Directory, show this quite plainly. The men's list includes 91 employed men and 3 retired men. Of the 91, 84 had jobs or occupations that fall clearly into the service classification: 29 porters, 27 laborers, 8 cooks, 7 houseboys, 7 janitors, 2 shoeshine parlor operators, 1 fairgrounds attendant, 1 laundry employee, 1 gardener, and 1 theater fireman. Only 7 men had jobs or occupations that do not easily fit the service classification: 3 farmers, 2 pastors, 1 teacher, and 1 contractor. (Even the pastors and the teacher can be thought of as being in service professions; however, their services were for Blacks rather than for Whites.) The women's list includes only 36 persons and is probably incomplete. However, all the jobs involved service: 12 domestic workers, 14 cooks, 7 laundresses, 2 housekeepers, and 1 boardinghouse proprietress. Of all these, only the boardinghouse proprietress served Blacks rather than Whites.

1945–1965

Many men of the Black community served in the armed forces during World War II. Some of them received specialized training that took them definitely out of the unskilled job category, at least during their service. Upon their return to Sequoyah after the War, they seem to have been determined that their economic status should not be the same as before. Some took courses under the GI Bill, seeking to improve their vocational and educational qualifications. Although few of them seem to have completed these courses, they did begin to move into increasingly skilled categories of work. They now work in jobs or at job levels previously closed to Negroes in Sequoyah, but most of them still work in the area of service, as broadly defined, and particularly in the automotive-service trades. The early stages of this change involved Black men working as porters. They say: "We swept our way into better jobs." Because of the pioneering of these men, now in their middle years, young men coming out of school find it possible to get jobs rather readily in the garages, although they do have to start out at unskilled levels.

Between 1945 and 1965 a good many women also took courses aimed at improving job skills; but during this period few of them were able to get jobs based on these skills.

During the same two decades, gradual changes were taking place in other areas of the social structure of Sequoyah. The Sequoyah Good Neighbor Council was founded and began to exert quiet but persistent pressure for civil rights; the University and the High School were desegregated; other Jim Crow restrictions began to disappear. These changes took place slowly. Nevertheless, there was more change during this period than during comparable periods of the preceding one hundred years.

Acceleration: 1965–1968

We now turn to a discussion of social and cultural changes since 1965. The pace of desegregation, integration, and job breakthroughs has accelerated markedly. To some extent this acceleration reflects nationwide trends in civil rights legislation, anti-poverty legislation, court decisions, and the rise of Black Power militancy. But local events were also important, if only because they translated national trends into concrete local action.

Three important events that took place in Sequoyah during 1965 were particularly responsible for triggering subsequent culture change. These were: (1) the decision to complete the desegregation of the Sequoyah school system by closing Carver School; (2) the workshop on poverty sponsored by the Sequoyah Good Neighbor Council; and (3) the special election in which Sequoyah voted to abandon the old mayor-and-council form of city government in favor of the city-manager form. So far, only the first two of these events have produced significant change in the culture of the Black community. The third has significantly influenced change in the city as a whole and, in the long run, will probably affect the Black community.

Grade School Desegregation

Sequoyah High School had been integrated in 1954 and the junior high school (seventh through ninth) grades had been desegregated, one by one, in the three succeeding years. But the six lower grades remained segregated for almost another decade. Some mild agitation for complete desegregation developed in the early 1960s; by no means did all of the Black people actively support it, though only a few actively opposed it. Some Black parents feared that the change would be especially disturbing to the very young children. Furthermore, Carver School was much more conveniently located for children living in the Spout Spring district than were any of the other elementary schools. But it was recognized that the change would have to come sooner or later; and most Black people realized that, in the long run, integration would mean better education for their children. When the change actually took place, it occurred smoothly. The only unpleasant incident that we know of involved some insolent comments by White boys in a junior high school when the former principal of Carver School was introduced as a physical education teacher and assistant coach.

In the three years after the integration of the elementary grades, there have been some problems involving Black children. Some have had trouble adjusting, both academically and socially. Some Black parents have blamed White teachers and students for this. It is hard to evaluate such charges. In some instances real malice may have been expressed; but we suspect that the charges are often rationalizations based on misunderstanding and lack of communication. The younger children have undoubtedly been subjected to considerable "culture shock" just by being introduced into a new kind of educational environment. Some of them have tended to be wary, and this wariness has apparently been interpreted as hostility by White children and, perhaps, by White teachers too. Other Black children overcame their shyness quickly and have adjusted well.

In general, it seems to us that teachers and administrators in the Sequoyah school system are aware of special problems resulting from cultural deprivation and are looking for ways of solving these problems. They may tend to be too "middle class" in their attitudes; but, as they point out, the American school system is geared to socialize children into a middle-class culture, and no other clear and practical alternative goals have been suggested. Therefore, they cannot see how they can be expected to develop such goals. They do recognize the need

Children playing in school yard. This school is attended by most Black elementary students. It was integrated in 1965.

to understand the initially non-middle-class habit patterns of children from low-income families. If anything, White children with low-income backgrounds are more deprived culturally than Black children in Sequoyah. This is so because they are generally less familiar with the "middle American" way of life than the Black children are. Two factors explain this: (1) the greater contact of Black families with middle-income White families through the domestic employment of Black mothers, and (2) the longer residence of Blacks in Sequoyah.

The Anti-Poverty Program

The 1965 poverty workshop resulted in setting in motion the process by which the Lincoln County Community Outreach Agency was established. This was achieved by a kind of liberal coalition made up of the Sequoyah Good Neighbor Council, the League of Women Voters, the Junior Chamber of Commerce, and organized labor. This same coalition also ramrodded the movement that resulted in setting up the city-manager form of government.

The COA has often been a center of controversy. But it has definitely influenced the economic and social status of Black people of Sequoyah. It has done so by example and by setting up training programs. The example has involved hiring Black staff members and integrating the agency's governing board, advisory boards, and committees. Vocational-training programs, other educational classes, summer Head-Start programs in Sequoyah, and the Child Care Center in Sequoyah are all integrated. All are aimed at social and economic integration of poor people in general and Black people in particular. Five Black graduates of vocational-training programs have obtained jobs in local businesses in work categories previously closed to Negroes. All five are women: one is now a cashier in a supermarket; one is in training as a telephone operator; the others are working as file clerks or receptionists in offices. Equal opportunity laws and regulations have certainly made these jobs legally available, but COA programs provided the necessary training. It will be remembered that during the period from 1945–1965 most job breakthroughs were made by men rather than women. Thus it appears that the COA has so far mainly had the effect of creating equal job opportunities for Black women. There have been job breakthroughs by men since 1965—a machinist, the COA neighborhood director, and further inroads into the automotive field—but none of these (except the neighborhood director) can be attributed to the COA directly. (Since 1968 at least five more women have gone into office work or related white-collar work, and one man has begun a contracting business in the construction field.)

Controversies in the COA

The Black community has been affected by controversies concerning COA policy within the larger Sequoyah and Lincoln County communities. There are close ties between Black families and university families, based on work and on interaction within the Sequoyah Good Neighbor Council. There are similar ties between Black families and native White families of the middle- or upper-income levels. Some university people became suspicious of their native White allies in the "liberal coalition." Apparently they felt that younger members of Establishment families were mainly interested in sponsoring change as a means of perpetuating control of power, influence, and wealth by the local elite. Power struggles broke out within the COA during the winter of 1967–1968. Both groups received support from friends in the Black community. Other Black people, like many university and native White people, reacted to the power struggle by withdrawing from active participation in COA affairs. However, the assimilationist leadership in the Black community tried to remain neutral and worked to restore some kind of harmony. They feared that continued conflicts within the COA would damage the agency's programs, which they value highly. In this they may prove to be good prophets. The local agency has recently been subjected to critical attacks by field representatives from the Regional Office of the Office of Economic Opportunity (OEO).

OEO attacks on the Lincoln County COA seem to involve three factors: (1) pressure from Washington to find ways of reducing rural anti-poverty expenditures in order to make more money available to riot-plagued cities; (2) panic reactions among OEO personnel resulting from the election of a Republican president in 1968; and (3) personality clashes between key OEO field representatives and top administrators in the Lincoln County COA. These clashes are said to have resulted after some local university-based dissidents allegedly met with OEO representatives and persuaded them that the local COA administration and governing board were not truly representative of the interests of the county's poor people. They based these charges on the low attendance at most area council meetings and other meetings of COA boards and committees. We are inclined to interpret this low attendance as an expression of the regional aversion to formal organization, which we discussed in Chapter 8. Until attacks began from outside, poor people seemed reasonably satisfied with existing programs. Their chief complaints were that there were not more of them. Since the attacks have begun, however, poor people have begun to be more critical, assuming that the attacks prove that there is something wrong. We do not mean to imply that the agency's administration and governing board have made no mistakes. On the contrary, we believe that they have made tactical and strategic errors at several points, sometimes as a result of overreacting to outside attacks.

The OEO Regional Office has just drastically cut funds for the COA and has imposed some rather limiting restrictions on its programs. The intent of these restrictions is to force the local agency to stimulate community action among poor people. It is difficult to predict what success such efforts will have, but we are inclined to the opinion that it will be extremely difficult, if not impossible, to build up and sustain in Lincoln County the kind of participation in formal meetings that OEO usually regards as evidence of community action.

Whatever future the COA may have in Lincoln County, it has already set in motion processes of assimilation and cooperation between Whites and Blacks that will probably continue.

The City-Manager System

The new form of city government seems to have had little effect, so far, on the Sequoyah Black community. To some extent it has weakened the voting power of Black people and of poor people in Sequoyah. This has occurred because all members of the City Board of Directors are now elected at large, whereas under the old system four councilmen were elected from the four wards of the city (with only two at large). Poor people in the south end of town had one person on the old council who represented them and who was dependent on their votes for election. Blacks are in a different ward and were always a minority in that ward; but they were at least a potential balance-of-power vote. Now, in the city at large, the Black vote is insignificant. In the long run, however, the greater professionalism of the city-manager system may be an asset to Blacks. City managers are career-oriented professionals whose reputations depend on establishing good administrative records. Since concern for the interests of Blacks is now paramount among municipal administrations in the United States today, it will probably be desirable for all men in this profession to establish good records with respect to the interests of Blacks. In this connection, the small size of the Sequoyah Black population is possibly an advantage, since it should be relatively easy and inexpensive to establish such a record in Sequoyah. So far, however, there has been no significant change in the circumstances of the Sequoyah Black community that can be attributed to the new form of city government.

The Urban-Renewal Issue

One possible future change could profoundly affect the Black community —indeed could bring about the disappearance of its present residential focus in the Spout Spring neighborhood. The Sequoyah Housing Authority, a semi-autonomous agency, has for some time been considering possible urban-renewal projects. Moreover, it has already begun three low-cost housing projects in the city. One of these is being built on the grounds of the old Carver School, which was sold to the Housing Authority by the school district. There have been rumors in Sequoyah during the past three or four years to the effect that one urban-renewal project being considered would involve the complete "clearing out" of all houses in the Spout Spring neighborhood west of Birch Avenue. They would be replaced by a park and a civic center, which would include a new Federal Building and a new County Courthouse. Further, a lake would be created by damming Forbes Branch. Most Blacks fear and oppose such development, and they have been supported in their opposition by a good many friends among Whites. The basic objection of the Black people is expressed in the question: "Where would we go?" None of the suggested or implied answers to this question are satisfactory to the Blacks.

Most Black families own their present homes but could hardly afford to buy homes elsewhere in the city with the money they might be paid in compensation for their present homes. Thus, most of them would be forced to rent quarters in the new housing project being built on the old Carver School grounds. Although the housing project must be officially integrated because Federal funds are involved, it may well end up as a largely Black tenement complex. It is hard to see how this could be prevented if most of the present Black-owned houses are torn down.

An earlier plan for disposal of the Black population is said to have involved a proposed housing complex to be built about ten miles south of Sequoyah, presumably as a kind of "back-to-the-country" policy. Apparently this plan is no longer being considered seriously.

Our last information concerning thinking in Sequoyah on this problem seems to favor a selective form of urban renewal: that is, only the worst structures would be eliminated; others would be preserved and improved through grants or loans to their owners. It is quite possible that there will be no urban-renewal project at all in the Spout Spring neighborhood. However, Black leaders are very suspicious of this present "lull," fearing they are being given a sense of false security so that they will be unable to form effective opposition to a later "clean-out" plan.

It is obvious that the continued existence of a distinct Black residential area in Sequoyah involves *de facto* residential segregation. A few local Blacks could afford to buy or build elsewhere in the city, but problems of financing would prevent the majority from doing so. A clean-sweep type of urban renewal in the present area would probably split the present community between a tenement population in the housing project and a scattering of Black small-house owners or renters in other parts of the city. The more selective type of urban renewal would probably preserve the presently segregated area. Poorer families would move into the housing project after their present homes were condemned; but at least two-thirds of the present houses could probably be spared and could continue to be occupied by Black families. Although an assimilationist point of view is probably held by the majority of Sequoyah Blacks, a majority would also prefer to keep their present homes.

Aspirations of Youth

The recent period of accelerated culture change (1965–1968) has raised aspiration levels among young Blacks beyond goals presently attainable in Sequoyah. Many young people reject domestic service or clean-up work as symbolic of inferior status. This causes older Black people to criticize the young people as lazy. However, these same older people are not necessarily satisfied with the *status quo*. Most of them welcome the prospect of better jobs and other improvements in the lot of Black people. But most of them also feel that, for individuals, improvement comes through hard work and the acquisition of necessary job skills. They have adjusted to lower economic goals than the young people will accept. But these goals have been attainable goals, for at least some people.

The higher aspirations of the young people cannot be dismissed as unrealistic. On a nationwide basis, White-dominated society in the United States has been moving in a direction that recognized the validity of such aspirations. Locally the Sequoyah community, which is predominantly White, has also been moving in that direction. The main difficulty, both nationally and locally, seems to us to be a lack of adequate means by which young Blacks can actually attain the goals they have set. In our opinion this is largely an economic problem. The kinds of skills needed in our technologically complicated society require expensive training. They also require a good educational basis, since the necessary training can only be obtained by people who are sufficiently educated to understand the training. Most young Black people of Sequoyah now have the chance to get the necessary education. Moreover, special job-training programs are available, though there are not yet enough such programs. Furthermore, not enough of the young Black people are going to college, although college is available to them in Sequoyah itself, as well as elsewhere in Ozarka. The cost of a college education is not beyond the means of most Black families of Sequoyah, especially in view of the various federally funded loan programs and work-study programs. The antipathy of young Black people toward the university is the main obstacle to their making use of this convenient local opportunity. There are now a few local Black students enrolled at OSU. If they succeed, others may follow. If some of that success involves participation in athletics, it will have great symbolic value.

If the present tendency toward a separatist ideology continues among young Blacks, their future will not be in Sequoyah. Sequoyah will now accept considerable assimilation. It will probably not accept militant separatism. In our opinion, there will be some young Blacks who will accept Sequoyah as it is—or as it is becoming. Others will probably go elsewhere to seek what they want.

Works Cited

FRAZIER, E. FRANKLIN, 1939, *The Negro Family in the United States.*
  Chicago: University of Chicago Press.
GREENFIELD, SIDNEY M., 1959, *Family Organization in Barbados.* (Columbia University doctoral dissertation).
  Ann Arbor, Michigan: University Microfilms.
KRIESELMAN, MARIAN J., 1958, *The Caribbean Family: A Case Study in Martinique* (Columbia University doctoral dissertation).
  Ann Arbor, Michigan: University Microfilms.
KUNSTADTER, PETER, 1963, "A Survey of the Consanguine or Matrifocal Family."
  American Anthropologist 65:56–66.
MOYNIHAN, DANIEL PATRICK, 1965, *The Negro Family: The Case for National Action.*
  Washington, D.C.: Government Printing Office.
OGBURN, WILLIAM F. AND MEYER NIMKOFF, 1964, *Sociology,* 4th ed.
  Boston: Houghton Mifflin.
OPLER, MORRIS EDWARD, 1945, "An Application of the Theory of Themes in Culture." *American Journal of Sociology* 51, No. 3, 198–206.
———, 1945, "Themes as Dynamic Forces in Culture."
  American Journal of Sociology 51:198–206.
OTTERBEIN, KEITH F., 1965, "Caribbean Family Organization: a Comparative Analysis."
  American Anthropologist 67:66–79.
RAINWATER, LEE, AND WILLIAM L. YANCEY, 1967, *The Moynihan Report and the Politics of Controversy.*
  Cambridge, Mass.: MIT Press.
SMITH, M. G., 1962a, *West Indian Family Structure.*
  Seattle: University of Washington Press.
———, 1962b, *Kinship and Community in Carriacou.*
  New Haven: Yale University Press.
SMITH, RAYMOND T., 1956, *The Negro Family in British Guiana: Family Structure and Social Action in the Villages.*
  London: Routledge & Kegan Paul, Ltd.
SOLIEN, NANCIE L., 1959, *The Consanguineal Household Among the Black Carib of Central America* (University of Michigan doctoral dissertation).
  Ann Arbor, Michigan: University Microfilms.

Recommended Readings

A. *Works on Black Subculture(s) in the United States selected for recency or particular relevance to this study.*

BROOM, LEONARD, AND NORVAL GLENN, 1965, *Transformations of the Negro American.*
New York: Harper & Row.
(Analysis of change in cultural and social characteristics of United States Negroes, especially during the past one hundred years. Emphasis is on summarizing sociological studies dealing with these matters.

BENEDICT, LONA, 1966, *The Process of Quiet Desegregation in a Small Southern City.*
(University of Arkansas, MA thesis).
Fayetteville, Arkansas: Department of Sociology and Anthropology.
(Probably the first published use of the term "quiet desegregation." Mainly an analysis of employers' attitudes, after the fact, to specific milestones in desegregation in an Arkansas city.)

CLARK, KENNETH B., 1965, *Dark Ghetto.*
New York: Harper & Row.
(Demographic and sociological analysis of social structures in United States Black ghettos, with interpretation and recommendations by the author, a distinguished Black social psychologist.)

FRAZIER, E. FRANKLIN, 1949, *The Negro in the United States* (Rev. ed.)
New York: Macmillan.
(A somewhat dated general statement by the noted Black sociologist. Frazier was long regarded as the sociological spokesman of Black society in the United States.)

———, 1957, *Black Bourgeoisie.*
Glencoe, Ill.: Free Press.
(A debunking of the myth of an important Negro middle class in the United States.)

HARRINGTON, MICHAEL, 1962, *The Other America.*
New York: Macmillan.
(A journalistic, quasi-sociological exposé of conditions in the "culture of poverty" in the United States. Credited with being the principal stimulus behind the Economic Opportunity Act of 1964.)

HERSKOVITS, MELVILLE J., 1941, *The Myth of the Negro Past.*
New York: Harper & Bros.
(An attempt to demonstrate that American Negroes have strong cultural roots in Africa. This thesis, strongly presented by the outstanding United States anthropological specialist on Africa and the Negro, was a challenge to currently held theory that Negroes "lost" their cultural heritage during slavery days. The Negro sociologist E. Franklin Frazier was the strongest spokesman for the "lost culture" position. Until recently, general consensus in United States social science tended to support Frazier's position, but there is a recent trend to reconsider the position of Herskovits.

————, 1966, *The New World Negro.*
Bloomington: Indiana University Press.
(A compilation of Herskovits' papers in the field of Afro-American studies, by his wife, Frances S. Herskovits.)

KEISER, J. LINCOLN, 1968, *The Vice Lords of Chicago. Case Studies in Cultural Anthropology.*
New York: Holt, Rinehart and Winston.
(The first book in this series to deal with modern Black society in the United States. It is essentially a structural study of an important "sodality," a neighborhood gang in the city of Chicago. Provides a striking contrast to the type of subculture described in this book.)

LEWIS, HYLAN, 1955, *Blackways of Kent.*
Chapel Hill: University of North Carolina Press.
(One of the best ethnographic studies of a Black community within a larger, White-dominated community in the South.)

LIEBOW, ELLIOTT, 1967, *Tally's Corner: a Study of Negro Streetcorner Men.*
Boston: Little, Brown.
(An anthropological participant-observer's study of Black men in Washington, D.C., who are refugees from the "matrifocal family.")

MORGAN, GORDON D., 1970, *Poverty Without Bitterness.*
Jefferson City, Mo.: New Scholars' Press.
(Brief sketch of the social and economic hardships of a Black family in central Arkansas. The author, now a professor of sociology at the University of Arkansas, records his own impressions of the life struggles of his mother, father, and grandparents, then uses incidents recollected from his own boyhood to illustrate how a nonseparatist, assimilationist position can be achieved from such a background of poverty and discrimination.)

————, 1970, *The Ghetto College Student.*
Iowa City: The American College Testing Program.
(Black sociologist's report on the characteristics of Black college students from inner-city ghettos in four major United States cities. The emphasis is on the distinctive strategies and tactics used by such students in dealing with (and often resisting) the teaching efforts of professors and administrators.)

MYRDAL, GUNNAR, 1944, *An American Dilemma.*
New York: Harper and Bros.
(The classic compilation of research on the American Negro conducted prior to and during World War II. The author was the director of the research program and uses a value-oriented approach to interpret the findings. This book was one of the major bases for the United States Supreme Court's school desegregation decision of 1954.)

PARSONS, TALCOTT, AND KENNETH CLARK, (eds.), 1966, *The Negro American.*
Boston: Houghton Mifflin.
(A compilation of special essays by social scientists dealing with the problems of current desegregation and integration of United States Negroes in United States society.)

YOUNG, VIRGINIA HEYER, 1970, "Family and Childhood in a Southern Negro Community." *American Anthropologist* 72:269–288.
(A report on field observations of children's behavior and of adult-child relations in a small Georgia county-seat town. Important for sweeping challenge to current concepts regarding the quality of Black family life in the United States. This author definitely sees the United States Black family as functionally efficient, though in a culturally different context than that of the United States middle-class norm of the nuclear family. Supports certain findings of the present study but in the context of a general Black subculture, whereas our emphasis has stressed the context of the local or regional subculture.)

B. *Readings on the Ozark Regional Subculture.*

BROADFOOT, DENNIS L., 1944, *Pioneers of the Ozarks.*
Caldwell, Idaho: The Caxton Printers, Ltd.
(Charcoal drawings of the individual Ozark old-timers, together with short autobiographical sketches of each, recorded in native dialect.)

GOODSPEED, 1888, *History of Newton, Lawrence, Barry, and MacDonald Counties, Missouri.*
Chicago: The Goodspeed Publishing Co.
————, 1889, *History of Benton, Washington, Carroll, Madison, Crawford, Franklin, and Sebastian Counties, Arkansas.*
Chicago: The Goodspeed Publishing Co.
(These are typical nineteenth-century United States county histories. The counties covered in these two books are all in the Ozark region, and the books definitely record the flavor of nineteenth-century Ozark rural and small-town life. They are somewhat hodge-podge presentations of demographic, economic, geographical, and historical data, intermixed with personal and family anecdotes dealing with prominent citizens or "characters.")

RANDOLPH, VANCE (ed.), 1932, *Ozark Mountain Folk.*
New York: Vanguard Press.
(Describes traditional Ozark lifeways and social activities.)
————, 1940, *An Ozark Anthology.*
Caldwell, Idaho: The Caxton Press, Ltd.
(Essays and short stories about Ozark people by native writers or interested outlanders.)
————, 1946, *Ozark Folkways.*
Jefferson City, Mo.: State Historical Society of Missouri.
(Collection of native folksongs.)
————, 1947, *Ozark Superstitions.*
New York: Columbia University Press.
(A four-volume compendium of Ozark folk beliefs relevant to such topics as weather, crops, livestock, water-witching, courtship, marriage, and burial.)
————, 1951, *We Always Lie to Strangers.*
New York: Columbia University Press.
(A collection of typical "tall tales told to tourists.")
————, AND GEORGE P. WILSON, 1953, *Down in the Holler.*
Norman, Okla.: University of Oklahoma Press.
(Analysis of Ozark grammar and pronunciation, as well as other aspects of the regional dialect.)

RAYBURN, OTTO ERNEST, 1941, *Ozark Country.*
New York: Duell, Sloan and Pearce.
(Tales, essays, and traditions of the Ozarks edited by Erskine Caldwell.)

STARR, FRED, 1958, *Of These Hills and Us.*
Boston: Christopher Publishing House.
(An account of the acculturation process undergone by a flatland teacher and his family after they moved to the Ozarks during the Depression. Emphasis is on culturally distinctive aspects of personality and customs, though presented in terms of adjustment to these by the author, his wife, and their children.)

SAUER, CARL OLWIN, 1920, *The Geography of the Ozark Highlands of Missouri.*
Chicago: Geographic Society Bull 7.
(An early work of the great United States cultural geographer, who was an Ozark native. Very good on geology, economics, history, and general landscape description. Surprisingly naïve cultural interpretations.)

WEST, JAMES, 1945, *Plainville, U.S.A.*
New York: Columbia University Press.

(One of the early anthropological community studies of a United States small town and its county. The location is on the northern periphery of the Ozarks. Gives a very clear description of rural and small-town culture of the 1930's.)

WRIGHT, HAROLD BELL, 1907, *The Shepherd of the Hills*.
Chicago: Book Supply Company.
(A novel dealing with a former minister who retires to the Ozarks and becomes a philosopher-mentor to his neighbors. Good for a vivid description of Ozark life and culture in the latter part of the nineteenth century.)

————, 1909, *The Calling of Dan Matthews*.
New York: A. L. Burt.
(A sequel to *The Shepherd of the Hills*. Good for analysis of small-town middle-class mores in the Ozarks around the turn of the century.)